My body was eaten by dogs

With the compliments of the Canada Council

Avec les hommages du Conseil des Arts du Canada

A Short Bibliography

Books

The Poem Poem, Kitchener, Weed/Flower, 1967.
The Saladmaker, Montreal, Beaver Kosmos, 1968.
Letters From the Earth to the Earth, Toronto, Coach House, 1969.
The Great Canadian Sonnet, Part 1, Toronto, Coach House, 1970.
The Great Canadian Sonnet, Part 2, Toronto, Coach House, 1971.
Poems Worth Knowing, Toronto, Coach House, 1971.
The Ova Yogas, Toronto, Weed/Flower, 1972
Intense Pleasure, Toronto, McClelland & Stewart, 1972
A Knight in Dried Plums, Toronto, McClelland & Stewart, 1975.
The Poet's Progress, Toronto, Coach House, 1971.
The Saladmaker (rev. ed.), Montreal, Cross Country, 1977.
On the Road Again, Toronto, McClelland & Stewart, 1978.
I Don't Know, Montreal, Vehicule, 1978.
A New Romance, Montreal, Cross Country, 1979.
A Trip Around Lake Erie, Toronto, Coach House, 1980.
A Trip Around Lake Huron, Toronto, Coach House, 1980.

Some Other Writings

"Drapes," (a story), *Quarry* XIX:3 (Spring 1970).
"Here Are Some More Snaps," (a story), *The Fiddlehead* 87 (Nov.-Dec. 1970).
"Premature Notes on Some Biological Effects of Poetic Composition," *Open Letter*, Third Series, (Summer 1976)
"It's a Funny Thing," Interview by George Bowering, *Copperfield 3* (1971).
"The Twilight of Self-Consciousness" in *The Human Elements*, (ed.) David Helwig, Ottawa, Oberon Press, 1978.

My body was eaten by dogs

Selected Poems of David McFadden

Edited by George Bowering

McClelland and Stewart Limited

Copyright © 1981 by David McFadden

All rights reserved. No part of this publication may be reproduced or transmitted in any form or by any means, electronic or mechanical, including photocopy, recording, or any information storage and retrieval system, without permission of the author.

ISBN: 0-7710-5500-5

McClelland and Stewart Limited
The Canadian Publishers
25 Hollinger Road
Toronto, Ontario
M4B 3G2

Published simultaneously in the U.S. by Cross Country Press

Printed and bound in Canada

Contents

Introduction 7
Keys 19

The Sixties

The Saladmaker 23
The Sky and I 23
Poem in Honour of Canada's 100th Birthday 24
Slow Black Dog 25
Bathing in Diabolic Acid 26
The Gnome Poem 27
The United Church Observer 28
Man 30
God, The 30
Overhead 31
Darryl and the Moose 31
Last Fishing with Jack 34
A Jewel Box 34
Another Mouth 35
The Cadence 36
She Wore 36
Fingers and Toes 37
After Lullaby 37
Tongue to Tongue 38
Tick Talk 39
Poem to Last for Seventy Years 39
Pop 40
Journey to Love 41
Did I Make My Body? 41
This Poem Has a Good Title 42
Sunday Afternoon at Home 43
A Lloyd Abbey Saturday 43
Judge Me by My Pantihose 44
A Sense of Danger 45
Making It 45
Cold Rain Song 45
The External Element 51

The Seventies

Orchard Suite	55
Visions of Old Hamilton	56
Polluted Shoreline	58
Chocolate Bars Can Fly	59
The Owl	59
Natalia	59
Alvin Munn's Wife	60
Alone on the Great Divide	60
After Thomas Hardy's "Afterwards"	61
Correction	61
The Spoiled Brat	61
A Typical Canadian Family Visits Disney World	62
My Criminal Record	65
Death of a Man Who Owned a Swimming Pool	66
Vibrations	67
U.S. Tourists	67
The Saint	69
Fairies	70
How to Become Part of Nature	73
Incident at Parrsboro	73
Low Tide at Noel	74
The Invention of Gunpowder	75
The Canadians and the Russians	76
Moose Jaw	77
The Angel	78
The Wound	82
A Knight in Dried Plums	82
from The Poet's Progress	83
Prince George Express	87
How I Came to Understand Irving Layton	93
For Barbara	96
The Rockies	97
My Body Was Eaten by Dogs	98
Hsu Fu's Speech to the 500 Youths of Both Sexes	100
Fingers	102
Border Skirmish	103
1977	105
The Opening of the West	106
Lennox Island	110
On the Road Again	112
Intense Pleasure	112

Proofing the World
The Poems of David McFadden

ONE SATURDAY NIGHT I sat with David McFadden in Maple Leaf Gardens, watching Toronto beat Detroit 6-0. At game's end, when sixteen thousand people began to rise & file out, McFadden opened his book bag & shouted, "Wait, wait, I have some poems to read to you!"

He was joking but he was not kidding. All his writing life he has acted as if the poem had a real function in the social life of his country & world, as if poems were composed by a human being intent on taking his part in the building of a place to live in. The poet is perhaps not the unacknowledged legislator of the world, but if the citizens could have their ears unstopt they would at least recognize him as a functionary. McFadden does not want to replace the famous athletes in the workaday dream machine; he just wants to take his turn with them.

David McFadden was born (1940) in Hamilton, Ont., & he lived there until 1978. Canada's biggest steel-producing city, Hamilton, half-way between Buffalo & Toronto, is the country's emblem for postwar working-class life. People who live there, one fancies, participate without choice in the life of hourly wage, producing the element of national "growth," & accept with no question of will the attendant despoliation of the ecosphere, & the avid leisure-hour invasion of the American trash culture. Under cast-iron clouds Hamiltonians in Dacron slacks go bowling, eat brown-coated chicken parts, & watch game shows on Buffalo TV stations.

But David McFadden's bungalow was on "Hamilton Mountain," a portion of the great Niagara Escarpment, a precambrian survivor of God's geography that almost joins Fenimore Cooper country to the Canadian Shield, that huge rock backbone of Canada, a symbol vastly important to our literary mythologists. Hamilton Mountain does not rear itself above the smog, but it insists on its priority; it tells the imagination that this part of the continent was all this high once, that the Niagara Peninsula & the Great Lakes were not always a flat stage for coke furnaces & Pepsi shacks.

The Escarpment is an important symbol for McFadden, but no more important as a base for his poetic than as a foundation for his house. McFadden did not go to university, but neither did he choose the idle life of some Canadian "working-class" poets. He was for a decade a proofreader for the Hamilton *Spectator*, & for several more years a reporter, chiefly on the police beat. Thus he was a wage-earner with words, & an artist raising a lower-middle-class family. Each night he drove down off the Escarpment into the dark of the mills, & in the daytime he wrote poems that took for their subject the lives of regular human beings, divine in origin but compelled to enact their lives in the midst of the trash era. As Frank Davey put it in *From There to Here*, "the message of McFadden's poems is that individual man inevitably is forced to participate in both the *lumpen* culture and global political forces of his time."[1]

One does not have to read far in McFadden's verse to find out that he's chosen to be a romantic poet in the line or company of Blake, Wordsworth, Shelley, Whitman & Kerouac. That choice implies a vision relentlessly connecting metaphysical belief & detailed concern for the quotidian fate of the least powerful people in his society:

> You would see him bobbing proudly along
>   Kenilworth Avenue
> dressed in ill-fitting pin-striped suit & flowery tie
> bought in a second-hand store,
>   his right hand bent in a perpetual wave,
> two paper bags in his left hand.

McFadden's poems abound with the crippled & the ill-used but the word that shows up most often when desire or appreciation is signalled is "perfect."

The ancient poets believed that perfection existed far from their world. Their Romantic successors wrote about the aspiration to find it, feeling its shadow in the hearts of human fools. Later it became a metaphor in the poets' store of figurative speech. The Moderns have mockt the idea, or rued the loss of its allure. But McFadden sees its gleam still, ready to put the lie to the Modernists' despair. He often follows the word "perfect" with the word "little," to be sure, but throughout his work one reads of perfection as a possibility, a hope, at least a wish, as the positive force that permits such a person as a working poet to seek a worthwhile alternative to the world of trash & murder.

McFadden quite agreeably adopts the Wordsworthian notion of human children arriving in the world as out of perfection, retaining the dream or memory of the divine state. Thus the maimed & oppressed are apt images for his major theme, the dialectic between metaphysical beauty & the trash culture. We see the crippled form divine, & the poet's mercy, pity, peace & love as hope of redemption of this awful life.

That hope is a very important theme for the lives we have to live after the realized despair of the Modernist era. Can divine hope, backlit as it is by twentieth century irony, serve to clean up our trashy world? For a time in the late seventies McFadden seemed to be trying to abandon his struggle by entering into a series of long metaphysical poems, but recent short works discover him among the interior mountains of British Columbia, attached again by personal disruption to the earth, whose letters he eagerly stuffs into the nearest mailbox.

Children, his own two daughters especially, have always best focussed McFadden's rays of sadness & hope, as others did for Wordsworth & Blake during the smokiest days & nights of the Industrial Revolution. In fact, more than simply associating children with innocence, McFadden has often identified the poem as a child. His first book, *The Poem Poem*, presumably composed during his wife's first pregnancy, equates the emergence of verse out of oblivion with the uterine flowering of a new human beauty. As every once-expectant parent knows, a developing pregnancy is a time for fantasy, the struggle to shape a dream, as the fact comes closer to being. In the struggle (see especially McFadden's more fantastic poems) the shaping imagination is either an escape from trash or a saving grace, an *action* that must be taken in a world where they want to deliver pizzas to your door.

A writer who often places his hopes on his own folk will be called "sentimental," & McFadden has been called that by critics who dont like to see grand statements hinted at in little stories of family life. I like what Ted Berrigan once said about Frank O'Hara's "personism":

> Any attempt by you to sum up what you're like is of necessity going to be a sentimentality, a piece of sentimentality. But to tell the world what *a life* is like, showing some life with an "a" in it, at the center and therefore the central character and therefore the hero, but a very funny kind of hero because not an epic hero, or not a tragic hero and not a romantic hero, not a proletarian hero, not an ordinary man hero, but not a put-down anti-non-hero, either. Rather, a human being, an "I"...he's writing, literally, plays...That's what's real about his poetry and makes it be like the poetry of *our* times.[2]

Somebody with the contemporary sense once did create out of McFadden's vignettes a Hamilton stage production called, I think,

"The Collected World of David McFadden." And McFadden has sometimes presented his printed poems as one-page plays. But they are plays, originally, acted for us every day, & the poet presents himself as audience, sometimes interlocutor. He is the twentieth century artist who allows a lot of light into the poem. He does not, as the normal American or Canadian academic poet does, seize upon a European statue & build a meditation to fill the space. He goes where the true mind bids him. "The open-ended universe opens in the middle," he wrote once, & the play we are watching is the play of air & light & mind around the figures thus discovered.

Such a mode of writing requires subtlety, & McFadden, though sometimes he gives in to a base pun, has from earliest plays shown a subtlety we pick up nicely if we remain tensile of fancy. For one thing he has always had a deft sense of notation, as for instance in the poem "God, The," in which he makes the most cunning trace of the mind among the quotidian. His is Whitman's ear (though seldom Whitman's mouth. And let me not suggest that I am citing WW as a maker of subtle prosody), listening to the world's parts making exclamations in his head. In his best short poems he likes to present narrations without obvious comment, in the faith that his reader also knows where poetry comes from. In fact he often seems to stop the poem before an expected punch line—Robert Frost with a witty pair of scissors. That is why academic Canadianists do not write about his work. A characteristic early poem is "November Fly":

> Into the bedroom—
> papers on the bed
>
> white-curtained window
> blind drawn down
>
> a fly walking
> November fly
>
> buzzing around the papers
> paper fly hovering
>
> disappearing
> at my approach
>
> but remaining
> in my confusion

  into the cellar
  looking at the

  dahlias, 9
  of them, getting

  ready for the
  winter, to be

  split in the
  spring, maybe

  making 36
  or 45, but

  they look
  weak somehow

  I don't know

  November fly
  confusion

  of my motion
  & things I know

which makes use of a subject familiar to all readers of English poetry. But McFadden does not allow himself to make the relativistic conclusions poets traditionally offer on the subject. He stops between "things I know" & "I don't know." (A decade later he titles a booklength poem *I Don't Know*, the words of wisdom put out by Bodhidharma to the Emperor Wu). Usually the poet musing on the fly is brought to make a remark on the fly-like life of a man, but in the language of an instructed & therefore wiser observer of life. McFadden takes the proposition further, & with the subtlety I spoke of, so that his reader has to begin to draw the conclusions about human life, & then draw back from that temptation.

 Sometimes the reader will feel herself invited to make conclusions but unsure that she really knows what the "product" should be. The compositional method that makes for such "confusion" or uncertainty is at the heart of McFadden's poetic. Often he will seem to offer implied comparisons of bits of information or events, giving only the implication of the comparison, not the spark that one wants to see leaping across the space between the details, the impulse, say, to settle the order implied in coincidence. It is as if, being the proofreader of God's pages, the poet should proffer only the clarity of the text, not an exegesis of it, not an interpretation. Borges, who proposes just such an occupation, puts it this way: "All poetry consists in feeling things as being strange, while all rhetoric consists in thinking of them as quite common, as very obvious."[3] You will have noted the aptness of the present participles there.

Thus it is that one comes away from an encounter with McFadden as one does from an encounter with his fellow artist, Greg Curnoe: unable, that is, to feel certain whether the man is determinedly innocent or guilefully parodic. McFadden acts as if fairies on tree-limbs are perfectly ordinary parts of the population, & as if a dog crossing a back yard is magic, as if universal world peace might be reported in tomorrow's paper, while a white hair in a mustache can arrest logic. "There is no difference between Grand Vistas & my everyday body." The world is filled with domestic numen. Thus it is important (see his poem on Thomas Hardy) to write every day, a little in a hurry or more on a long afternoon, to pay for, to use each day.

So to the mind eager for rhetorical instruction the details seem to declare only their own significances, as in a painting, though in a syntax that are trained to read for widening meaning. In one of McFadden's poems the colour red shows up all day, & it is with a little conditioned restlessness that the reader will find that the poet does not then make a generalization on the message carried by the colour, as countless university-journal poets would. In my favorite McFadden poem we find a (I almost said "perfect") sly instruction that reads both to & from the McFadden manner:

> Barbara, put down your flute
> and pay attention.
>
> A motorcyclist in the high Andes
> has been forced off the road
> and is falling...
>
> Quick!
> Do something!

There is a relationship between the poet's decision not to draw conclusions (unless they be transparently preposterous ones) & his interest in little perfections. We cannot be familiar with the perfect, & interpretation makes for familiarity. We cant be familiar with the perfect unless we are perfect ourselves, & being perfect we would be silent, being perfect we would be saints & therefore still wherever people are moving. In his poems McFadden is always seen as a regarder, moving. In his earliest poems he moves around Hamilton, its corner-stores & buses & bowling alleys. In his second phase he is seen travelling about Ontario, observing people at lake resorts or gas pumps. In more recent times he has taken the whole of Canada (& the odd vacation in the U.S.) as his subject, purposefully making books that collect his little plays set in Nova Scotia or British Columbia:

>   *Toss*
>   *a dart at the map of Canada,*
>   *where it lands is*
>   *where you'll find me.*

That means that he is (a) the map of Canada, (b) pinned by a dart, or (c) a dart thrown at the map of Canada. I think that all three are more interesting than one of the more recent professor-critic ideas: Canadian poet as map-maker.

A name for McFadden's art, observation rather than interpretation, is collage, arguable (Donald Barthelme so argues) the main mode in our century. One critic[4] has noted collage & its effect in the big-little novel, *The Great Canadian Sonnet*, with its left-hand pages by McFadden & right-hand drawings by Curnoe, & in *Letters From the Earth to the Earth*, thru which the domestic poems share unnumbered pages with snaps from the McFadden family photo album. But the rest of his books are collage too. If one sets his little plays in a twentieth century Canadian city such as Hamilton, one has chosen a stage that is itself a collage, where in walking down a street one walks by a Greek pizza parlour, then a Chinese cafe, then a Korean martial-arts gym.

For that reason, because of his interest in disjunction & mindscatter, McFadden does not employ much rime in his poems (except, again, the obvious ones made for parodic purposes), because rime would seem to suggest orderliness that proclaims authorial control of a world. The collage of the visual out there coming in seems to provide a more true imitation of the world so surprising in its multiplicity. Fragments of a city life, as they appear to eyes & ears—at first the poems seem unended or unworthy of beginning, & they do not bring the ease of repeated sounds. They are no more resolved than daily life. They are not a mesh but rather snapshots that form just a collage from whatever time (tempo) permits. A longer poem, "Meaningless Midnight Musings" (from *Intense Pleasure*), brazenly records whatever comes to the poet's consciousness, & admits throughout that a poem is being collected:

> A poem is a hex to prevent repetition.
> Freedom from the cycle of birth & rebirth.
> Her blouse was all undone. Her breasts
> smelled like butter.

From the poem emerges a poetic, not the other way round, emerges a belief that God edits your life & your job is typesetting, proofreading.

In the seventies we see in the poems more & more construction of scenes, fewer innocent snaps; the collages are synthesized of outside & inside. At the same time, the vision becomes darker, little lamb replaced by the hungry tiger. McFadden was reading Jung, & mining his dreams, presenting the latter as concretely as possible, trying to pass them off as plain-faced reportage. "A Typical Canadian Family Visits Disney World" gives a sense of the new direction in its bipolar title, & throughout illustrates it with a core of the mimetic wrapt in metaphorical exaggeration (elsewhere called hyperbole) & irony:

> The girl at the Detroit bridge asked if we had any oranges
> & it was snowing in the United States of America
> & the snow was much cleaner & fell more neatly
> than in Canada, & there was more of it, Ohio
> looked like a Bing Crosby Christmas card.

"The Spoiled Brat," one of my favourite poems, in which the poet-narrator tricks the title character into a surprise decapitation, is presented as just the latest of many anecdotes about life in the McFadden house. It is delightfully & constrainedly an encasing of wicked emotional fantasy. Such comic malice reappears in "Houseplants" (Mrs McFadden teaches their care), in which the poet tells of the nasty way he took advantage of the discovery of the plants' sensitivity to human behaviour. In other poems a dream woman turns into a fanged monster, a selfish homeowner dies of shock beside his invaded swimming pool, a stone talks incessantly of its decapitation, enough to make one yearn for ditties of no tone. Yet the sentences are simply declarative, so that we are convinced that their author is yet as he was, staying away from interpretation, quietly & candidly collaging the days. Collage is much more interesting than simile for just that reason, because the latter leads the reader to respond: well, everyone's entitled to his opinion. Opinion? says McFadden, "but I am fearful/of being in error."

It is right that we should still see the enthusiastic, encomiastic young poet, & the gathering of skill, never at the expense of early poetic, thru the enclosure of darkness that makes itself appear more authentic on the outside edges of that early light. McFadden has grown to such stature that he displays because he began so openly; he was not just another youngster who equated poetry with the ability to contemplate violence with smug horror.

But if McFadden's plays of experience show a pain that was only posited in his plays of innocence, it is not because he has changed his ideas on what is true. Blake's "Songs of Experience" do not cancel his "Songs of Innocence" any more than the New Testament cancels Moses. We have to die, & we have to grow up, & growing up includes being able to read *thru* newspaper stories instead of just from top to bottom. In his poems of the seventies McFadden does not so often speak of his dream of changing history thru poems, but rather announces that he does not mind the trash invasion because poetry's work goes on, "the work/ of simple people learning how to sing/ with the help of the Fairies," so "if you believe as I believe/ & have seen strange things you've feared to speak of/ please write me care of my publisher." Now that request is loaded with mockery, mainly because the publisher is there in between, but if one did not care, why bother?

Whereas the McFadden over twenty used to speak in Emersonian terms of "error," the McFadden over thirty holds his eyes & mouth open to cruelty:

> for there are mysterious people in the world
> who steal children & kill them
> & stuff them in holes in the ground

And he tells of it with his habituating comic syntax & structure. Now even children partake in what seems natural, inborn cruelty:

> The crazy castrated cat called Al
> sat crouched in front of a brick wall
> as if about to leap
>   through it
> while slowly a crowd of kids
> gathered to watch & jeer
> hoping to see him crack his skull

What McFadden is giving us by his simplicity of view is not a guileful picture of an innocent abroad in a sometimes crummy world—in this later period he offers quite a number of poems that show the lyricist as poorly behaved, too. But he wants to stay away from the narrowed observation of the confessional poets, who tell their readers why they feel as if it is an unpleasant life. McFadden's aim, admittedly futile but gallant for all that, is to compose like the world, not its observer:

> To write involuntarily
> as mountains are formed
> as ice grows on peaks
>
> as forests clothe the slopes
> directly
>   instead of only after
> hasty study of the proper methods
> of producing work merely mimetic
> of the involuntary mind

When he seems to do that his audiences at readings enjoy themselves. McFadden's public readings are more enjoyable than most because they provide relief. Even when he tells stories of murder, evisceration, childhood agonies, listeners smile at one another, laugh till they fall down, nod their sad heads in full agreement. They are hearing a total human person, a cynic who finds life pleasurable, an ascetic who fondly shares his appetites. They are listening to a man who reminds them of how two horses stand together in a springtime field, but does not claim that his observation sets him apart. It is as if he is saying look, the earth gives you all this & it is too easy to forget it. He acknowledges heroes, but no great heroes. He candidly revels in his ability to make poems but he does not ask anyone to interpret his little plays into works of high drama. In one of his earlier poems he said he was happy to recognize his poet-self as "a minor God, but nevertheless God."

Therefore of use. In the sixties he averred: "There's nothing for man but art and earth/ and no hope but in seeing." The first line echoes medieval division of the world, & the second is a terse & handsome reason for making art in the post-existentialist age. Of his poems from that period the young McFadden advised, "Take them in loaves as for lunch." That is a good line, because it combines the humble with legitimate Christian pretension. It assembles the poet's convictions—bread & poetry are sacramental, but bread is bread, after all, modest daytime fuel.

Thus the title of the book introduced by those three lines: *Letters From the Earth to the Earth*. Loaves, letters. The title refers not just to poems (or to Mark Twain's position), but to human lives as letters that are delivered to their original address. That early, & still today, McFadden is a comic metaphysician, but the working poet reminds us where we live, what our poor bodies are made of & the messages they carry in their transit. Of "poemology," a mystery to his ordinary wife, he wrote, "It grows under her feet/ & lines her stomach."

"Infinity needs you, son," he reminds himself then, but the statement is an echo of a line from a western movie, in which a frontier town is trying to recruit a marshall. If John Clare had had a sense of humour he could have been a wonderful early David McFadden. Note the return in these two lines: "the vacuum at the end of the imagination/ the amazing ground of laughter." But it is essential to a reading of McFadden that one feel sadness & terror downstairs while one is laughing at one's face in the bathroom mirror. His great preoccupation, children, live in a world of beauty & love, & are closer to death than to poetry. Poetry is an activity derived from experience, *is* experience; it feeds on the innocence of children, keeping itself alive, like a man living on blood transfusions. See "A Jewel Box" or "To Elizabeth Ann Fraser," & try to keep laughing. All the poems are indeed love letters to the world, as natural as eating & peeing, but they carry the message of conscious care & the knowledge of probable destruction: "the flower of the world/ bullet-riddled."

But as the earth continues to make flowers & children, it does so without mawkishness or misgivings; so one continues to make poems, knowing them to be mortal from the beginning, not knowing how the world is going to use them. There is no market research save in the trash business. "Keep going God," wrote McFadden in the late sixties. "You've/ got the right idea." Despite the trashing of Vietnam & the shooting of Martin Luther King, sheer plod makes plow down sillion shine. Maybe.

In the context of this kind of place, the best way to read David McFadden's world is to read thru it all. You will find "little perfections" from time to time, & they will accumulate, spots in time that happen so often that you will entertain the notion that we *can* be saved. You will see that McFadden often admits a desire to write the perfect poem, but fills his verses with the unavoidable signs of mortality under this earth's veil. Anticipating eternity, he is haunted by time, past & future, his own & the world's. The statue of a knight fashioned of dried plums is a criticism of marble statues, but it is also not food. Cats, dogs, turtles & budgies are invited into the poems to be with the people there. If the world is space, & living a life is time, then David McFadden is like so many Canadians a travel poet. But unlike the others, he does not wind up sitting back in his chair to look & see whether you got the point. In the later & longer poems especially, there is a word that becomes more important than "perfect." It is "and."

"And" is not a word that leads one to dance around a figure; it is in terms of meaning, concerning the relationship of events in the world, a letter that will never get down to "yours truly," quite correct. It does not allow a "therefore." In the long poem, *The Poet's Progress*, McFadden, on entering the second half of his life, examines his process as a poet, as the formerly neglected arises, & says of his career, as Yeats might: "we/ can never know our warm, leafy/ surroundings but can only be them." Not imitators but constant creators of the world.

George Bowering

[1] Frank Davey, *From There to Here*, Erin, Press Porcepic, 1974, p. 184.
[2] Bill Berkson & Joe LeSueur (eds.), *Homage to Frank O'Hara*, Bolinas, Big Sky, 1978, p. 214.
[3] Willis Barnstone, "Thirteen Questions: A Dialogue with Jorge Luis Borges," *Chicago Review*, Vol. 31, No. 3 (Win. 1980), p. 12.
[4] Ronald Kiverago, " 'Local Poet Deserves Attention': The Poetics of David McFadden," *Open Letter*, Third Series, No. 5 (Sum. 1976).

My Body Was Eaten by Dogs
Selected Poems

Keys

*Wanting to write a poem, I
walk around all day with the
tips of my fingers wide open*

touch   touch   touch

a star at each tip

*and run home, let them press
into the keyboard*

The Sixties

The Saladmaker

Joan is making salads
and slowly
         the knife

flashes for a perfect
moment
          as down it goes

through the cucumber
for all time

through the kitchen walls
reflected in the sun

through the human
flesh
     of the saladmaker
     her lovers
     her children

and through the cats
wrestling on the floor—

The Sky and I

I'm paying my mother a visit,
walking towards her house
and the road, usually smooth
and open, has become broken
and partially closed, barricaded
by crews of construction workers—

On my left they're laying new sewers,
on my right an old graveyard
is being ripped out for the foundation
of a new apartment building,
and they're piling up stacks of old
caskets, groaning in the sun,

sad old cosmic caskets in rows slowly
moving along a makeshift conveyor belt
past a blazing incinerator
into which their contents are dumped,
then moving on into the casket factory
where they are refinished
and resold for reuse—

But I manage to pass through
and visit with my mother for an hour
then return the way I came,
chat with the sweating workmen
in fact ask little questions
about the age of the graveyard,
height of the proposed building—

And the world is full of sunlight
and I am full of spiritual light
walking along like that
and the sky is full
of mild electrical powers
as inside me I feel
springs going off

and the sky and I
are full of a voice, saying

      PREPARE NOW FOR DEATH

as I continue walking,
thinking what a good idea.

Poem in Honour of Canada's 100th Birthday

I'd planned to get a movie camera eventually
but I got one earlier than I could afford
because of the centennial parade

and when the parade started up
the fucking camera wouldn't
and there won't be another centennial parade
as you know for a hundred years

so listen Steinbergs Miracle Mart
and all lovers of pure poetry
I want my money
back

Slow Black Dog

Meditating in the back
of Jack's green Volkswagen
rolling along Highway 2
east of Paris

I'm conscious only of the motion
of things speeding against me
on both sides of my head,
eyes closed, and a sudden braking

and a breaking of that dream.
I'm in a moving car among green hills
and cow grazings of the world,
motels, gas stations of Ontario

and a dog slowly walking across
into our speeding lane, a black dog,
and in tall grass at roadside, a boy,
waving his arms, screaming.

Bathing in Diabolic Acid

It was a voice on the phone late at night
saying I understand you need a new rear bumper for your car
and later I drove through the rain. And my car
was caked with mud, clumps of weeds
blooming from the tailpipe. And even later
with my daughters washing their hair
in a warm house under great heaving thunderstorms
I solemnly wrote a cheque for ten dollars.

These are mediocre moments in a mediocre life
as I bathe daily in diabolic acid.
And I hope I have not bored you
with details of a life you'll never live
being sick enough with your own.
But oh it ain't so bad. Whenever I'm bored
I bash my forehead against the typewriter
as if it were a perfect little image of the world
as it was on the day I was born.
And somewhere it was raining and someone
was driving to the wrecker's in an old car
covered with mud. Don't wreck that car, I shout.
In 20 years it'll be worth a great deal of money
on the antique market.
                    The moments,
how much more would they be worth?

Further, I have a pair of slippers in my mouth
and a little yellow knife in my heart.
The moments are perplexing me, my lines
have suffered a certain decomposure.
You should have cut it off six lines ago
yet it strikes me as poor form for a poet
to refrain from writing while uninspired.
Anyone can write while inspired. It takes
a master poet to write while uninspired.
Take me for example. When inspired
I have better things to do than compose.
When dull and dry, my normal state,
I write to evoke inspiration
and when it's invoked I quit

and during that gentle swing from A to B
my silly little heart breaks with joy.
Oh, I love it. Oh, I want more and more.
Oh, I never want it to end.

Someday I'll write a big book on prosody
so everyone will be able to avoid writing like me.
It's so difficult. We all talk with the same accent.
We all eat Big Macs. We all agree
poetry is the hard bottom of the lake,
the bed or rock that will never feel the hot
touch of the sun in our lifetime. It would
have been a mysterious death. It will always be
a mysterious life, plenty of rocks
to sun on in sunny Ontario or Quebec.

The Gnome Poem

I took some film of a
beautiful girl in mauve
brushing her hair

(on a beach this is)

and an interesting brown dog
sitting nearby
              walked over to the girl
who stopped brushing her hair
and began brushing the dog's,

all into my film,
thin transparent coiled strips
of these moments moving forever
inside who knows what other moments.

The United Church Observer

Night breezes blow through the bedroom curtains,
my wife is asleep and the cat awake at her feet
and me awake with my notebook, the breezes,

the cat cleans its fur with a felt-tipped tongue,
jumps up on to the window sill,
blumps, bumps clumsily into the screen,
a woman's body in sleep turning

into my notebook because someday
all these things will be dead

and I'll curse myself for not having
recorded these images

and the murderous world draws its desire
out of its desire
           and with age
we find the world's not a globe
but a two-dimensional circle among many

for I am Adam and my screams
drown out all others, the song
of the language of my pointed moment
protecting me from putrefaction:

the cat is getting too frisky
and is about to awaken my wife
and so I light my cigar butt
and blow smoke in his face,

the cat calms down, concentrates
on his claws, Joan is peaceful
as an unpeeled banana.

Some cosmic splendour greater than Marx or Christ
nudges at me and many others I know of
and everyone I suspect

and everyone has a different version of it.
It enters the language of each differently
giving its subject the Voice of Authority—

What could it be?

It makes us intimate and loving before it
sets us to murder each other,

into my notebook because I want to know it,
or other versions in complement with mine.

I don't want to know it.
My trend is to the front
of the brain.

Go to hell big vision.

Or, come to me you're
bigger than I am.

The little visions will suffice
till you come crashing in.

No one I ever heard of
ever chaste a big poem
though I guess lots did.

Can you use ordinary motor oil
on a squeaking clock?

The cat crawls up on
Joan's belly, Joan
wakes up,

Bloody cat, she says,
throwing it to the
floor,

relaxing

and reaching for me.

Man

I'm sitting on the floor
watching TV, big space walk,
blood brother spaceman,
flesh and blood lover in space,
astronaut like yogi in samadhi
tumbling over and over at the end of his
spine, I mean line

        and Alison
coming close, pointing to the tube
asking
    "Feeeeesh?"
and me with prideful resonance
answering
     "No. Man"
            mind rushing on,
            having
                second thoughts.

God, The

coffee is good this
morning, and the sugar

and the cream, and
Joan
    paddling around
    (a Sunday
morning, this) talking happily
about TV,

        makes me think
I am the immortal Don Quixote
gone sane,
        and Joan, she

is Spain.

Overhead

I come out of the bathroom, a
lion, after haircut, hair
plastered down, thin and wet

the budgie, hovering
over my head, afraid
to land.

Darryl and the Moose
   (for Al J. Plant)

      I

There was a fat kid in there,
about 12, with a bottle of pop
and a chocolate bar, leaning
against the cooler,
              and I said
Excuse me, opened up one side
of the cooler. Just big bottles
in there, so I closed it, opened up
the other side, looking in, pausing,
hesitant.
        So the kid said What kind
are you looking for? And I said O
no particular pop, just whatever
looks good,
            then grabbed a Grape Crush.

As I opened it, two women, in their late
forties or so, walked in, flashing
big smiles at the kid, saying
Hello Darryl, then talking to the
woman behind the counter, softly,
the kid straining, listening like mad.

It was hot in there, so I dropped
12 cents on the tray and walked out.

Standing in front of the store,
taking swallows of pop.
                    I'd had
enough when half finished, but didn't
want to take it back in like that,
so I finished it off, walked in,
plopped the empty down on the cooler.
Mom, said the kid, interrupting
the woman's chatter, you owe
this man two cents.
                    And she
got real flustered, looking about,
confused, then rang up the register,
smiled, put down two cents, saying
Thank You.
              And I flipped the pennies
and caught them, walking out past
Darryl. Just as I passed him I
winked,
          with a little smile.
And he smiled. God, did he smile,
little fat kid.

         II
Next door was the Moose Hall, and
on the step was sitting an old man,
nice cleanlooking old man, the janitor
I thought, the doors open behind him.

I said Do you work here? And he said
Yes. And I said Do you mind if I use
your washroom? And he said Sure, it's
right down the stairs on your right.

And it was black down there, I couldn't
see a thing. So I came back up,
said Where's the light?
                     And he
answered It's just inside the door
on the left wall, about chest height,
well, you're taller than me, about halfway
between your chest and your belt.

                            So I
found it OK, and peed. And there were
some posters on the wall advertising
the Moose Lodge, and Mooseheart Village
and other things about the Moose.

Later, I was asking the old guy about
Mooseheart, and the posters, and the Lodge.

Mooseheart is a wonderful place for kiddies,
he said. It's just outside Baltimore.

Who can join this Lodge? I asked.
O anybody, just anybody, he said.
It's interdenominational, he said.
(I thought that was a pretty big word.
It wasn't on the posters.)
Anglicans, Presbyterians, even Protestants.
Doesn't matter about race, creed or religion.
Anyone can join. Anyone. But no niggers.

Whaaat? I said. In Canada?

The headquarters, he said, is in
the States, and when they say no niggers
they mean no niggers. I've been in
this Lodge for 52 years, he said,
and I didn't know about this till
just last week. I was wondering
why we never advertise our dances,
so I asked Ken (the bartender). And he
told me that if we advertised the dances
we'd get niggers, and that's against the
rules. Headquarters says no niggers.

He was a real nice old guy though,
sitting on the step, in front of the open doors,
late midsummer afternoon 1966 in Hamilton.

Last Fishing with Jack

Jack wore his brown sports car cap
and me my gold star cowboy hat
and we stopped the car in the graveyard
crumbling slowly down into the gorge
between Southampton and Chippawa Hill.

I carried my rod and the tackle box
and Jack his rod and the bait basket
and the path went almost straight down
maybe a hundred feet
into the last rapids of the Saugeen
before it enters into Lake Huron
there in that strange gorge
rimmed with a crumbling graveyard
filled with the music of the rapids
music that goes on and on
down where the river divides into three
for a mile or so, leaving
two grassy treeless islands
and we waded to the first
and then to the second.

There in pools among the rapids
we pulled out four small bass
and took them home for eating.
Down we went into the empire
of the last rapids of the Saugeen
forever, and brought it home.

A Jewel Box

The little girl was ten.
I imagine she said
"I'm ten and drowning"
as the lake folded over her
layer upon layer, wave
upon wave, sun upon
sun, perfectly,
separating her from things

squeezing out her connections
swallowing all that power.

Maybe her brain's last picture
was of her jewelry box.
I hold it in my hands, now, with fear.
It's the girl's drowned head:
painfully handcarved, lost.
Mocking human love. And
something of the dead girl
comes up inside me
moving me with love
to love that jewelled box.

Another Mouth

Only six days old, Jennifer—
she doesn't even know her name
but radiates a pure intelligence
that expresses a flash of gratitude
when her big sister of three
drops a flower
in her crib—

An hour later she
spews three ounces of curdled milk
down her mother's dress—

For all my life I felt so alone
and now suddenly I'm split in four—

I sit smoking a cigar—
Alison walking past my chair
stops for a moment, looking up
in frozen recognition—
like a Canadian tourist in the bronze shadow
of the Daibutsu Buddha of Kamakura—

My slightest movement is charged with importance—
the sparrows come in and out of my nostrils,
building nests in the hollow womb of my brain.

The Cadence

Joan is upstairs
reading
       "a stupid book"

and I'm downstairs
preparing 140 poems
of the last year
for publication

and every hour
I go upstairs
to say I'll only
be a few more hours
and to hear old Joan say
"God this is a stupid
book."

She Wore

that dress when I was first
mad for her like a dog the moon

the dress of green flowers
green flower dress I used to wear

and now tries it on and my god!
it shrunk she says

but I ain't giving it to (slim) Irma
(who said gifts oblige) she says, throwing

it in the corner, me burying an urge
to pounce on it and bury it

like two
dogs two

bones.

Fingers & Toes

Poems coming out of my hand—
out of my fingers and toes.
No matter how bad, my best
at this time and place, and true.
The music moving inside me,
coming out, covered with language.
Earth noises, murmuring of life
touching life, nature selfreflecting.

Who wants the poems?

If you want them take them, friend.
I be crazy to make them,
you be crazy to take them.
Take them in loaves as for lunch
and our fingers and toes will touch,
our bloodstreams one, as they are
surely in reality.
                    Touchings like this
seem good to me. Teaching ourselves
all we know, from the depths. And
maybe The Gods can be reminded
they made us in their own vision
and when we wake up in the next birth
we'll find ourselves blessed, and singing.

There's nothing for man but art and earth
and no hope but in seeing.

After Lullaby

Sleep, sweet baby-blossom, like the
grass and vines. Hair growing,
fingernails growing, moon-
cells
      of bone and muscle
                        groaning

moaning sighing dividing dying.
Sleep and grow, sly bamboo-baby.

Sleep all night and when the sun
comes in the window I'll come and
get you
          and our brains will be
all bright again and we will have

breakfast, and
study the eggs.

Tongue to Tongue

Listening to Joan's voice
all moist and superripe
the vowels, bowel vowels
listening to the vowels

 and the upright consonants
—towns on a map.

Listening I sip my tea
chew a cookie slowly
—then roll a smoke
listening with my eyes

fingers toes and elbows
listening with my tongue

Listening to the vowels!
Hark! Erectile consonants!
She's got apple pies
in the oven, and cookies

vowels and ancient consonants
flying tongue to tongue.

Tick Talk

"I study her face so carefully
every day because she's changing so,"
says Joan, about the child,

my stomach moving slowly,
April sunlight from the window
touching Joan's face in ways
I never saw before.

Poem to Last for Seventy Years

Saturday morning, 1968, waking up
        one by one, the family
from dreams of death to Big Rocker
        B.B. King all day on the radio
and Joan's coffee

        —Michael Ondaatje the living legend
was here last night, the kids
        slept through the visit.

An old photograph has turned up
        of my mother's paternal grandparents
and this is my morning to look at it:
        The Pidgeons of Cardiff, 1898, forgers
of my flesh and they knew it, scowling at me
        over forty years before my birth.

The print is still in good shape and I wonder
        about those clothes: fine floor-length gloomy gown
an impeccably pressed vested four-button suit—are they somewhere
        still in some kind of ragged shape?
But I am shocked, my hair stands on end
        by that seventy-year-old instant scowl of dust.

The kids are awake, blinking. They sniff in corners
        for traces of Ondaatje,
a little remnant dust, a scowling glow.

Pop

I open the door and walk in
and little Alison comes running towards me
she has a limp yellow balloon in her hand
and she asks me to inflate it, daddy

It's almost bedtime and she
is wearing her pink nightgown
candystriped white and pink

and the balloon has printed on itself
in neat little type
FIGHT CYSTIC FIBROSIS
GIVE A CHILD THE BREATH OF LIFE

I blow the balloon up and the type
increases in size about ten times
(goes quickly from little to large)
(grows like magic)

(it would be nice if books
came in adjustable type
and nice if I could blow myself up
into John Keats' size

I've been reading John Keats

one day John coughed on to his sleeve
a little blood, he was 24
and knew death was nigh
[149 years ago this month]
so he wrote a letter to each of his friends
saying I'm going to die now)

I tell Alison to keep the balloon
away from the cat and she says why?
and I say 'cause the cat'll break it
and you will cry

A little later I hear from the kitchen
that characteristic POP of a burst balloon
followed by no crying.

Journey to Love

No one knows his own potential for evil
but yesterday Joan asked me to get us
a couple of Cokes

and I got a Coke for me
and a Diet-Cola for her.

"I resent this, I really resent this,"
she cried, sipping at her sweetness.

And today, forgivingly, she asked
if I'd written any poems recently

and I replied yes, "but they're too deep
for you, you'd never understand them..."

Did I Make My Body?

I saw birds flying edgewise in strong updrafts,
rolling hills, sloping earth, woods, a bay,
I could see forty miles in every direction,
everything was lit—

       pecking at this typewriter
       skillfully

           Dark overhead
   red sky in the west

      A big jet lowflying with lights blinking

I owe it to my kids to get a UHF converter

There is no difference between Grand Vistas
and my everyday body.

This Poem Has a Good Title

I was thinking of you
and wrote a handful of poems.

I'm a poem specialist!

More poems to write than tears in the ocean
sad to think I'll never get most of them written
especially the good ones

Maybe I should just specialize in good poems
No, I could never stoop that low
I want to work among the humble poems
poems that can't afford the high cost of justice
the havenot poems that don't know where to turn

But there's so many of them!
Who's next?
Jesus it's hopeless.

Maybe I should just specialize in titles.
Instead of writing 10,000 poems this lifetime
I should write 100,000 titles

I'm sure people would understand
and would be strangely grateful

and if all the poets gave up writing their daily poem
and started turning out something like 100 titles a day
—if there's a million poets in all languages
that'd be 36½ trillion titles every year—

Maybe something glorious would happen to the world.

Sunday Afternoon at Home

I was reading Alison a story from her story book
and Joan's father was horsing around with little Jennifer
and Jennifer's got nice whole white gleaming teeth
so "what pretty teeth you got Jennifer" said old Sid

while Alison's because of countless early respiratory infections
involving high fever and requiring antibiotics
are a little bit stained, holy and stumped

and Alison gave me a big beautiful smile and said
"I got pretty teeth too, see, haven't I daddy,"
and then before I could answer added in a softer tone
"Brown is pretty isn't it."

A Lloyd Abbey Saturday

"It's a bugger when a fellow breaks down on the road."
   —old guy sitting on his Highway 7 verandah

Watching Saturday afternoon football on TV
  while downstairs nutty Lloyd Abbey reads and writes,
    a self-tortured Wagner/Beethoven with a misunderstood difference

    The kids want to go down and play with him
    and I'm a little jealous—

Soon he'll be punching his palms
  reciting his poems
    waving his arms

      the kids roaring with laughter
      my hair standing straight on end—

Judge Me by My Pantihose

Ichiyanagi has found several efficient ways to free his music from the impediment of his imagination.
   —John Cage

Little Jennifer is always hurting herself,
just now as I watched
she turned and walked into a post
and caught it with her forehead,
two minutes later she bent down
and caught her soft nose on the big toe
of the foot of my crossed leg.

She has a lot of bruises

- one above her left eyebrow
     halfway to her hairline

- a half an inch behind and one inch below
     the left corner of her left eye

- two inches above the above

- one and a half inches right of the right corner
     of her right shin

- a whole constellation of them
     on her right shin

Under her clothing she's bruiseless
as the clothes provide natural padding.

Don't worry about that natural.

I should let her run naked,
get an allover bruise
     (no strap marks).

John Cage really makes me mad
with remarks like that above.

A Sense of Danger

Knocking around in the basement early Sunday morning
in a foggy hangover trying to remember my name

I bumped into the old birdcage
—the little door was down—
and I started looking for the bird
sensing he was in some danger

then my name came to me
and I remembered the bird
had been dead two years.

Making It

John Cage was on the radio
and in his dainty Frodo voice slowly and clearly
was saying

      "I went to visit my Aunt Marge..."

      with a little tinkle of pianos

      and Alison came into the room saying
      "What's that s'posta mean?"

Cold Rain Song
Nov. 2/69

Season of dry leaves and cold rain, squeaking tricycles—
Five days ago it was Halloween eh dad?

The road at Albion Falls is being straightened out.
New-cut earth turning to mud and sliding—

Joan stripping thick old yellow paint off an old stool, it's
going to be repainted white—

In the cellar Alison has her tricycle upside down
spinning the big front wheel by hand.
"I'm pretending I'm making popcorn."

"Watch this dad watch this or you'll miss it!"
I look. She jumps up two steps of the staircase.

Phone rings. It's Joan's mother.
Alison goes upstairs and comes down with a glass of apple juice.

She spills some apple juice—
I give her a rag to wipe it up.

She tilts her head back draining glass of juice,
her right eye wide bright blue pupil looking at me.

She wants a glass of water so I get her one from the
laundry taps. "Lucky we got taps down her eh dad?"

Upstairs Joan's talking enthusiastically to her mom
and I hear my name mentioned and something about Five Dollars.

Downstairs Alison pours water into the spinning wheel of her tricycle,
then wipes it up from the floor with the rag.
"Look how shiny it is now dad" (the floor)—

Upstairs Alison wants more water—
She pushes a chair across the floor to the sink
and gets the water herself—

Where'd they get that idea about making popcorn?
I don't know but I used to do it when I was a kid says Joan.
So did I. That's all I remember about my tricycle.

Joan is now working on her stool and yelling at Alison
for making a mess with the water.

Joan remembers she had a little red CCM tricycle
and stresses it was second hand. All I remember
was mine was CCM. I tell her mine was *third* hand.

Was it now, says Joan.
Sure, and when I finally got my first two-wheeler
it was a thirty-year-old monster my dad bought from my
mother's brother-in-law for Five Dollars.

Joan finally admits her Mom and Dad saved and scrimped
and bought her a brand new two-wheeler for passing grade 6.
It was a CCM too. A blue one. That was the summer
she had poison ivy but persevered and learned how to ride
so she could chase boys.

Just then Alison riding her trike zips right over Joan's finger.*
"Ouch! Hey! You ran over my finger stupid, watch it."

Joan is working hard at the stool. In two minutes she's going to say
wish I'd never started this job.

So in two minutes she says it
and I show her what I wrote.

Alison gets her little doll buggy and pushes it around the cellar
at a dizzying pace as Joan works away
then lets it go and it smashes right into Joan's rear end.
Joan grabs it and pushes it hard at Alison and says How do *you* like it?
and Alison cries a little bit.

Then faintly Jennifer crying from the bedroom upstairs.
Joan sends Alison up to see how she is and to give her a cookie.

Joan's cousin Valerie and her new husband Don
have no furniture and no money.
We're going to lend them our love seat for a few months OK? says Joan.
And I say OK, sure. And Joan's embrace and big kiss
of thanks for my generosity make me feel not so generous.

Mask time, says Joan. Start the mask will you please Dave.
I was just going to light up a smoke.
Can't smoke at mask time.

---

*For an account of Joan's foot being run over by a camper van see *A Trip Around Lake Huron*.

Joan's peeling raw carrots whole.
I'll have one of those I say and grab one.
No, I've only got three says Joan and grabs it back.

Alison is singing a song about Jacqueline.

Joan is tossing raw onions and carrots into the modest roast beef.
I manage to grab a small sliver of carrot.

I wash out the mask in warm water and plug it in, tests OK—
Fill up the receptacle with buffing compound (3cc) and Celbenin
  powder (1 gm.)—

Jennifer is running around the house like a magic cannonball.
Joan gets down on the floor and wrestles with her.

I get a football game on TV—U.S. game,
Philadelphia Eagles and New York Giants—

Montreal Alouettes are at Toronto today but blacked out on local TV.
Are you breathing deeply I say to Alison and she says yes.

She's singing a song with the line, "Bring me the helicopter."
Also she's reading her copy of Hilary Knight's Mother Goose.
She ignores the football game on TV but checks the commercials.
By the way, it's Philadelphia 13 New York 6.
It's cold and raining at Yankee Stadium too. Muddy sweaters
but not as bad as it used to be years ago now with new
  field-care techniques.

I look out the window and watch two girls walk by in the cold rain.
They stop and take off their shoes and socks and then continue on.

Wow! A blocked kick. Slow-motion replay, then a commercial
for Chevelle SS396.

Jennifer is wearing a red long-sleeved turtleneck sweater
and a double diaper, bare feet.

Alison has on her red buckle shoes, white socks,
green stretch pants, matching green sweater with yellow tulips—

Now it's a commercial for a 1970 Nova.

Joan grabs Jennifer and puts rubber pants over her diapers.

Philadelphia gets a field goal.

My eyes are sore from the onions and so are Jennifer's
(she's rubbing them) but Joan says hers are OK and so does Alison.

Jennifer grabs my poem and almost makes off with it, laughing.

I won't talk if you're going to put everything I say into a poem, says Joan.
I only put down the stupid things you say, I say.

Oh you're cruel, mean, sadistic and hopeless, says Joan.
What's hopeless, says Alison.

New York gets a TD. Philly 16 NY 13. Sure is muddy. Third
    period over.
I haven't got the energy to put on the radio to hear how the
    Canadian game's going.

Alison's chasing Jennifer around the house with her pants pulled
    down (Jennifer's).
It's hard to run that way but she does it.

Victor Coleman would be annoyed by the way I'm writing this poem
and yet he says maybe Blake is irrelevant.

Speaking of Art, this morning on TV they had some filmed shots
of the opening of the Sacred and Profane show at the Art Gallery
    of Ontario
and they interviewed anonymous people in attendance.
Mostly a bunch of phonies except for one guy they interviewed
and I looked again and it was Barry Lord, old J. Barry Lord of
    Hamilton
with his beard shaved off, saying this show is sick,
interest in this kind of art is a sign of deep sickness,
all this crap should be stuck in the cellar—
(Barry would probably love what I'm doing here)—

The kids are now eating apples and watching me write.
The camera team apparently didn't recognize Barry, formerly
editor of *Artscanada* and now editor of *Five Cent Magazine*.

Alison asks me to put her shoes on—
I say how come they're off?
She says I don't know. Hey dad is my hair getting long?
I get her shoes on and Jennifer comes around
and bites Alison on the left foot, almost breaks a tooth—
Guess she thought Alison still had her shoes off.

Five and a half minutes left in the game and there's been a lot
   of action (more than in the poem)—
Lost track of score. I think Giants have taken the lead.

Barry probably wouldn't be ashamed any more to admit he was
born and raised in Hamilton where you either play bingo or bowl
because now he's a big social realist and despiser of effete
   aesthetics
but I was talking recently to Mitch Cadeau who is from Hamilton
and now lives in Toronto and I said half the people in Toronto
come from Hamilton and are ashamed to admit it
but secretly Hamilton has really contributed a lot of brains and
   talent to Canada
and Cadeau gives me a meaningful glance and gives his friend a
   meaningful glance
and says I'm not ashamed to have been born in Hamilton but I'd be
   ashamed
to say I still lived there—

One minute and one second left on the clock. Forty-five seconds.
Fran Tarkenton trying to salvage the game
and Philadelphia intercepts with seventeen seconds left.

Final score Philadelphia 23 New York 20.

Cadeau said he'd been reading my book of poems and it brought back
all his sickening feelings about Hamilton.
I didn't know him when he lived in Hamilton but he says he knew me.
And he knew Bill Davies the Yogi who's a good friend of mine.
And he says how is Bill and I say he's just suffered a very
   serious heart attack
and Cadeau gives his friend another meaningful glance and says
remind me to give up yoga and she giggles.*

---

*Both Davies and Cadeau died shortly after, Davies from complications
following his heart attack and Cadeau in a car crash.

Toronto is leading Montreal 22-11 in a mud and fog bowl.
A meaningless game, Montreal can't make the playoffs.
Stupid series, every year the four eastern teams go through
the whole series just to eliminate one team.

Jack Fraser's Men's Wear is having its 43rd Anniversary Sale.

Jean-Paul Desmond will not be denied not even by death
in the new TV series Strange Paradise.
Henceforth I am God on this island. Bravo.
Just like I'm God in this poem.
A minor God, but nevertheless God.

Aromas from Joan's roast-beef oven fill the house.

The External Element

When I was a kid
I had kites and they always
ended entangled in trees

but stronger than the kite memories
is a dream I had at the time
in which my mother climbed a tree
to retrieve one of my smashed kites
and I cried out: "Ma, don't bother!"

And up there she lost her balance
and fell, landing across high tension wires
and was electrocuted, black cinder
of my mother falling softly to the ground.

For weeks after I couldn't do enough
to help my mother.
                    I was an ideal son
for over a month.

                    And even now
I hate poetry with a passion
and write poems.

The Seventies

Orchard Suite

I

Miles and miles of fruit trees
    have been cut down
to make way for these houses, each one
    full of happy children.

II

    Ladies and Gentlemen: the word for the deity of
whom I have heard so much throughout my long childhood
years at Sunday School could start with no other
letter than "G."

III

    There is a hole in the centre of my heart through
which God can be seen. Out of Him through that hole
Creation has spilled.

IV

    It is now impossible to get away with making the
same speech in every town. One must be completely
open or completely shut.

V

    When I press a certain spot on my chest I am
filled with joy.

VI

    The neck of my stomach is directly behind the level of the
bottom of my rib cage.

VII

I offend most people with my niceness. Occasionally,
however, I deeply annoy someone with my rottenness. There
seems to be no happy medium for me. Perhaps my niceness
is an effort to compensate for my thorough rottenness.
But then really who cares? Why should I care?

VIII

Boy, he really knew himself!

IX

In my head
Is my heart,
I am dead
In my art.

X

Discuss the blind in pictures.

Visions of Old Hamilton

I

Through the sky drifted a yellow balloon, a large illuminated
   cross hanging from its basket, and it seemed to be following
   Major Bateman as he ran, cape flowing, through the streets
   of old Hamilton.
Suspended with tiny pebbles the large dark waves of the bay
   received him as he ran off the dock at the foot of James Street.
Curse you curse you! He shook his fist at the balloon as he
   fished himself out of the water, rubbed the tiny pebbles
   from his eyes, and wrung out the cape.

Subdued but still angry Major Bateman stormed back to his
   office, occasionally looking over his shoulder and
   spitting an ugly oath at the softly following balloon.

   II

The major finally succeeded in creating fish in his old laboratory
   over the pool room at Balmoral and Cannon,
a little school of about twelve, all different colours,
and he was hurrying down to the bay to dump them in before they
   died.
He bicycled on the boardwalk because the roads were so muddy.
He passed two old friends who were out of work and looking for
   handouts—
The major thought he better hang on to the money he had, it
   might come in handy,
he never even considered giving them the fish. He rode out
   on the dock
at the foot of James Street and dumped in the fish.
The fish looked up at him through the clear waters and smiled
and each fish had a silver dollar in its mouth
and there were stacks of five hundred dollar bills floating slowly
out from under the dock like miraculous little rafts.

   III

Major Bateman lifted the manhole cover at the corner of Kenilworth
   and Britannia.
The water flowing through the sewer was unusually clear. Through
   it he could see
huge ugly blind prehistoric fish, dozens of them, each one obviously
   capable of devouring a fullgrown man,
but at the bottom of the sewer, sparkling like memories of childhood,
were dozens of huge gold coins. Characteristically, Major Bateman
   didn't hesitate.
He dived in.

Polluted Shoreline

I

Went on a car rally today with Jack,
went through six counties: Waterloo,
Wentworth, Wellington, Perth, Dufferin, Grey—
now midnight, drinking beer, Joan watching
an old British movie on Cinema Six, me feeling my hair
all greasy and dusty, eyes sore, telling Joan
about Garry Lee-Nova, how I bumped into him by accident
in Stratford, about his mirror waterfall
and kids breaking it as he predicted—
He probably paid the kids to break it says Joan.

I get a new beer, check the turtles—
they look on in silence, sleeping, water clean.
Jack couldn't stand the people at the rally today:
"I keep getting farther and farther from these people
and did you notice when the Molson's balloon went sailing over
they all ignored it?"

II

One a.m., drying my hair, Jenny running through the house,
Joan still absorbed in 30-year-old English movie,
nightclubs being bombed in the blitz—
I have to be hard at work in a few hours;
so much work to do in the next few weeks
I won't have any time for writing—sorry,
but I just had to mention that.

But everywhere I went through the six counties today
I saw people with time to write poems.

Chocolate Bars Can Fly

Chocolate bars can fly,
a wrapper lying on the ground
means a bar is soaring in the clouds—

wrapper sadly waiting its return.

The Owl

One night an owl
flew through the beam of our headlights—

for hours after we got home
the baby was awake.

Natalia

The tiny turtle named Natalia languidly swimming
    in her ten-gallon aquarium—
filter, pump, landing platform,
    gravel, clear water,
splash, dive, glide, surface, float, slowly sink—

I know I take unusually good care of the
    happy little amphibian,
spend hours watching her,
take her out in the back yard for the sun,
take her out for dinner and give her a little
    piece of my Big Mac, and so on.
But when the old lady is not around
Natalia undergoes a strange transformation,
rises out of her aquarium, becomes
a soft sweet warm 16-year-old
with green eyes and slips into my bed.

Alvin Munn's Wife

Alvin Munn's wife died.
"I pleaded with her to go to the doctor's
but she wouldn't listen," he told the cops
a month later when they broke into his apartment
to investigate the smell.

There she was sitting at the table,
a plate set before her,
strips of green flesh
falling from what had formerly
been her face
onto her plate—

"Why didn't you report her death, have her buried?"
a lawyer asked him later—
He hesitated a moment or two or three
then said, "I don't know,
I need help, I'm sick"—

No matter how simple, every question they asked him
he would hesitate a few moments before answering—

There was nothing spontaneous about him—

Alone on the Great Divide

No stance, no pose,
no pants—

An early morning quiz show on TV—
Name the film for five points—

Suddenly in front of me a child
becomes a fish, a horse—

After Thomas Hardy's "Afterwards"

After I'm dead
and time
continues on without me
much as it did before I was born

a child will pick up
a piece of dog shit
and eat it

and someone will say Look!
McFadden was a man who
would have noticed that.

Correction

Three motorcycles
were parked diagonally at the curb
in front of 111 Brucedale Avenue.

The Spoiled Brat

I couldn't stand the little bugger. He
was a spoiled brat. But his mom and dad
were always nice to me. So when they
asked me to mind him I said okay—

About 10 o'clock I picked up his dad's
rifle and pointed it at the kid. "I'm
going to shoot you, Bruce," I said,
and he ran in the corner and started crying.

He didn't notice me pulling out the shells.

Then I pointed the rifle right at his nose

and pulled the trigger. It just clicked.
He stopped crying and smiled.

So then I made a big show of loading the
gun again and then I told him I was really
going to shoot him this time and he began
to cry again and I pulled out the shells
without him seeing me again but I guess
I must have left one of the shells in
because when I put the gun under his nose
this time and pulled the trigger the gun
went off and he fell to the floor with
half his head blown off.

A Typical Canadian Family Visits Disney World

The girl at the Detroit bridge asked if we had any oranges
and it was snowing in the United States of America
and the snow was much cleaner and fell more neatly
than in Canada, and there was more of it, Ohio
looked like a Bing Crosby Christmas card.
We passed eighty jacknifed tractor trailers
and a thousand cars abandoned on the roadside
between Detroit and Cincinnati. Fourteen egg trucks
slipped off the road and crashed down hills
coming to rest balanced on the banks of roaring rivers
with no one killed and not an egg broken.
Our car stalled in the 90-mph lane and we never got hit,
I set out on foot leaving my typical family to freeze to death
and when I returned they were singing The Marten Hartwell Story.
We drank Pabst Blue Ribbon and ate spare ribs in the hotel room
in Lima Ohio and watched Archie Bunker on TV
and there was a party of black folks talking jigaboo lingo real loud
in the next room and someone pounded on the door
and one of the kids answered and said Mommy,
one of the jigaboos is here.
All the way down it was like being in
all the Hollywood movies ever made.

We passed the house Judy Garland lived in
during the filming of Wizard of Oz,
we saw an old wrecked fence
left when her house was tossed somewhere over the rainbow.
Pretty hills in Ohio were covered with snow,
frankly much lovelier than the Land of Oz.
We turned off our windshield wipers at 60 mph
and tried to commit suicide like Frank Sinatra
in Young at Heart but we hit a soft snowbank.
The town Marlon Brando was born in was flooded out
and people were paddling around in canoes with their belongings.
We stayed in the same hotel where Katherine Hepburn
and Spencer Tracy first spent the night together.
We passed a mental hospital on fire, corpses
being dragged out, the same hospital in which
Zelda Fitzgerald died.
In Kentucky the roads cleared up and the sun came out
and the forsythia bushes were in sweet blossom
making me sentimental for my Old Kentucky Home.
We passed a river Mark Twain pissed in.
We drove up a hillbilly road to a mountaintop in Tennessee
where B.B. King killed himself when he was only three.
I shot pool and drank beer in a pizzeria in downtown Knoxville
with Phil Ochs and the Veterans of the Vietnam War, the smell
of sweet wild onions and apple blossoms and violets filling the air,
flowering dogwood and jasmine floating in the breeze.

Sunset over the smoky mountains of the Cumberland Gap
with a full moon rising much larger and faster
than it ever rises in Canada.
One of the boys showed me a jar of gallstones
that once belonged to Thomas Wolfe.
Randall Jarrell's cousin Clellon took us for a ride
in his powder blue Caddy with white leather upholstery
and let us make long distance calls all over the world
and wanted to fly us to New Orleans for a shrimp dinner.
A young black guy in overalls looked at my plates and said
now there's a car I reckon's a long way from home.
We stopped for eighteen-cent hamburgs and met
Tennessee Ernie Ford who looked at us and said
Hello Sweet Things. We drove through a long series
of Civil War towns in the Confederate States and swore
at old black Uncle Toms driving horse and buggies and waved

at an old black guy sweeping the boardwalks
of rural Georgia. Pastel neon signs and palm trees
and four-dollar motels built in the reconstruction period.
In Valdosta Georgia we stayed at a motel built by
Doc Holliday before there were any motor cars
and I dreamt I had an eye transplant
and Joan dreamt of ghost families in the false ceiling.
I phoned my brother from White Springs Florida
where Stephen Foster wrote about the Swannee River
and Homer the red-haired cook who served us grits
complained about the hippies and the Interstate Highway
ruining the tourist trade, we looked at the old caved-in
White Springs Health Spa where F. Scott Fitzgerald
spent a couple of summers round about 1927.
Who could forget the fabulous Stephen Foster Tower?—
From up there you could see 100 miles along
the fragrant dreamy Swannee that Foster never saw
never being farther south than Poe's Richmond but so what?
In Orlando we saw the house where Jack Kerouac's sister
killed herself and also where Jack himself later died
mysterious and lonely among the white beaches and pastel teeth.
We bought dozens of free live alligators that turned out
to be skinks which we let loose in endless orchards of orange trees.
We met a good old New Brunswicker in Plant City who
is the manager of Fundy National Park, two Canadians
in January lying on the grass under the blossoming palmettos
and reading shitty little newspapers about gangs of blacks
holding up and murdering gentle sweet-hearted 17-year-old white
grocery clerks working their way through college. All the
blacks I see are nice folks who know their place. In the morning
this black guy with a cigar goes in all the rooms picking up the
tips before the cleaning women get there. Every day
barring massive power failures there is at least one typical
Canadian family visiting Disney World, and on this one day
it was my proud family, a nice place to visit if you get there
early to beat the crowds and there are special ways
to get free tickets for all the expensive rides and I applied
for a job as public relations man but they have a rule
against hiring any non-Americans except Germans.

Well, a lot of the stuff there reminded me of Canada,
the ferry boat was just like that one in Toronto bay,
Walt Disney himself was Canadian, or his parents were,

Peter Pan was a Canadian, the Wild West was Canadian,
Jules Verne, Jungleland, Hall of Presidents, Cinderella—
Later we drove to the pastel beaches of the Atlantic
and hit a place called Moon Slander, the I dropped off the sign,
within view of the launching pads of Cape Kennedy,
and all the kids cried about the Mickey Mouse Orchestra
and even me and the wife got choked up and held hands.
On the way back we went to an intellectual motel
called the Congress Inn in South Carolina with Toulouse Lautrec
posters on the walls all done in red white and blue.
In Washington we stopped to help a stranded motorist
and he was a French Canadian scared we were
going to mug him and we did. That's all folks.

My Criminal Record

Fined $50 for ejaculating on the step of the Planned
    Parenthood Clinic
Fined $10 for trying to stuff a $20 bill into a
    coffee machine
Fined $2 for molesting a policewoman
Three months in jail for accidentally touching a hitchiker
    on the knee while shifting gears
Fined $200 for lending my pen to an ambulance attendant
Suspended sentence for cutting my daughter's fingernails
    in a public park
Six months probation for chewing gum in a fire hall
Fined $49.50 for sniffing the base of a fire hydrant
A week on the psychiatric ward for signing a false name
    in a funeral home guest book
Sternly reprimanded for crying in a laundromat

Death of a Man Who Owned a Swimming Pool

In my bathing suit and sunglasses
carrying a portable radio
and a large bottle of Quick Tan
I walked into this guy's back yard
on Mountain Brow Boulevard
He'd never seen me before
He was sitting on a lawn chair
with a gin and tonic
as I put down my stuff without a word
walked out on his diving board
and plunged in

swam around for about ten minutes
climbed out
dried myself off
turned on my radio
put on some Quick Tan

The guy just sat there looking at me
Oh hi I said as if I'd just noticed him
I hope you don't mind me using your swimming pool
I haven't got one myself
Sure a hot summer we're having eh?

The guy didn't say a thing
He had a red face
and it was getting redder
and it wasn't sunburn

I think I'll have one more swim before I go
I said and plunged in again

When I climbed back out a few minutes later
the guy had fallen out of his chair
and was lying on his face on the patio

I turned him over
He was dead

Vibrations

I pretended I was a magician
and performed some clever card tricks for the kids
and now they are whispering about magic
and looking at me strangely

as once I fooled a group of poets
with my finger on the ouija board
until their hair stood on end
thinking the dead were speaking through me

And perhaps the dead do speak through me
but what does that mean?
Only that I am getting heavier with age
and soon will be among them

And it is a sign of my boredom, my failure
that I wonder if when I am among them
I'll be trying to speak through the living

For the world screams there is no magic
and the children having forgotten the tricks
kneel before the television

while because of my peculiar position
on an isolated angle of the world
I see our vast complex stupidity

and share it fully
and like the dead try to speak
through these tricks

U.S. Tourists

When you see cars with U.S. plates
roaring along lovely narrow winding treelined Highway 3
you pretty well know they're not really
    visiting Canada

but just using it as a shortcut
between Buffalo and Detroit.

Old whitehaired Stewy Lacrosse used to operate
    a gas station on Highway 3
and he's a little bitter about visitors
    from South of the Border.
Says he: "Every goddamned one of the stupid
buggers carries a bottle of whisky and a
revolver under the front seat."

I was westbound on Highway 3 at 60 mph
    heading into Tillsonburg
when a car with Michigan plates
    zoomed past me carrying a boat
and trailer which was weaving dangerously.
Suddenly a beer can went flying out of the driver's
    window
and hit the shoulder like a paratrooper
    landing in the Mekong Delta.
Then all hell broke loose.
The trailer weaved too far,
hit the shoulder and broke apart.
The boat slid one way into a tree,
the trailer smacked into a rock.
The driver screeched sideways to a stop
and as I sailed past him
he directed a furious Humphrey Bogart look
at me as if it had been *my* fault.

In the mouth of the historic Nottawasaga River
    near Wasaga Beach
my fishing line became entangled
    in the propeller
of my little borrowed motorboat.
As I toiled to disentangle the mess
I was knocked overboard by sudden waves
from a highspeed luxury cruiser
manned by flagwaving U.S. tourists.

A family from Illinois was staying near us.
The little girl and boy were continually fighting.

Every time my kids went out to play
the little boy told them to get off the street.

You might think it unfair of me to talk like this
and you would be right
but this kind of talk is justified
by unfairnesses much more momentous—

I am genuinely pleased to see U.S. tourists
    motoring into my native land
and my only hope is that they will return home
    safely
before too many Canadians are killed
or too much land is bought up on lovely lakefronts.

The U.S. tourists who remain here
are the ones who bother me,
the ones that are gradually filling
more and more influential positions here
and the ones that are buying up more and more
Georgian Bay or Georgia Straight islands.

I think they want to start
the whole damn experiment over again up here
and I would rather starve than see that happen—

The Saint

Last night I dreamt I was reading
obituaries,

my wife's, my children's.

Only when I came to my own
did I wake up in a cold sweat.

Fairies

We are caught in the nets of wrong and right
We are caught in the nest of outward order
Our hearts are worn out if not dead
And so we do not see the Fairies
said young Willie Yeats in 1901

And so he condescended to roam the wild countryside
collecting tales of the Celtic Fairyland before it died

And he found that Canada, Australia, New Zealand
are full of the descendants of those
who left Ireland to escape the Fairy Curse
whose glowing hearts that gave them grace to see
have now been replaced by TV.

Folk art is the soil where all great art is rooted
said young Willie Yeats in 1901, refusing
what is passing, clever, trivial, vulgar, insincere.
And a sincere young painter and poet I once knew
travelled throughout Canada for several years
collecting information on people and their art
and perhaps he spoke too much of what he had found
for his discoveries were stolen and put on TV
where they were mocked, insulted and blasphemed
by those who don't know they are blind.

I don't mind when the blind make war on the blind
for still the work goes on, the work
of simple people learning how to sing
with the help of the Fairies
said young Willie Yeats in 1901.

"We want to know if people still believe in Fairies,"
said the city editor to me, a naive cub reporter.
And so I had to go into the street and stop people
and ask them if they had ever seen a Fairy.
After a couple of days of this I discovered
that Fairy means something else in modern language.
Of 438 people stopped in the street
422 refused to discuss the question.

Of the sixteen who talked, nine admitted
having seen flying saucers periodically,
four admitted having experienced astral projection
but none would admit having seen a Fairy.

At a garden party in London England in 1801
the poet Blake was sitting beside an elegant lady.
Have you ever seen a Fairy Funeral? he asked.
I have, and they used a little leaf for the bier, he said.
The woman quickly changed her seat.

It is well-known that only fools such as Blake,
simple people with untroubled minds,
can ever hope to see a Fairy
although the Fairies reputedly inhabit
every land from the Equator to the Poles
and are more numerous than the rabbit.

Once and only once did I see Fairies.
I had fallen asleep in the garden and half awoke
to find the lawn the scene of a huge battle
between the armies of the red fairies and the blue.
"So there are Fairies after all!" I said (to myself)
as I looked harder and the battle faded.

Basically an educated man and no fool
although my mind is often ridiculously undisturbed
(even in these horrible times)
I realize the Fairies do not really exist
except as projections of the simple mind.
But I think the red fairies won that war
for two little girls I know have each reported
seeing female Fairies in red gowns,
one flying through the air,
the other sitting under a tree.

Another girl I know, aged 25
and married to a millionaire,
says she often sees Fairies
when she walks in the woods—
Fairies of all colours, except blue.

And a woman I know in her thirties,
married to a postman, used to see
black Fairies frequently.
She considered them Angels of Death
and they were calling her to her doom.
They would appear in the distance
wearing black capes and hoods
patiently waiting for her
and she by an act of will
hardened her heart
and forced them to disappear forever.
Perhaps they wanted her for her purity
and when her heart turned hard
they abandoned her.
And so she lost her life
although she saved it.

I am now forced to admit I lied a while back.
From certain angles I see angels
and I have seen Fairies often in dream and vision
and have often seen the hand of Fairies
snapping branches off trees I was about to prune,
hiding things and making them reappear in strange places
and I've heard them call my name
and I've heard their lovely music.

I believe my belief is shared by many
who because of natural fear will not admit it.

And so my fellow Canadians
or anyone who hears these words
if you believe as I believe
and have seen strange things you've feared to speak of
please write me care of my publisher.

How to Become Part of Nature

Pay your bills promptly
Keep track of everything you spend
Take taxis everywhere you go
Avoid people you're naturally attracted to
Discuss the weather with strangers
Make random phone calls at 2 a.m.
Neither apologize nor forgive
Avoid curiosity
Always wear blue suits
Never smile
Tell long boring stories
Yawn when people are talking to you
Avoid sex whenever possible
Complain loudly about unions
Cultivate a British accent
Make obscene gestures at nuns
Never fart in public
Rattle change in your pocket
Flush newspapers down public toilets
Lecture people about smoking
Collect pornography
Be the first to pass out at parties
Debunk current fads
Keep your eyes unfocussed

This is all you need to know. Within three years
of following these rules carefully
you will be part of nature.

Incident at Parrsboro

Dick Elliott the famous song writer
was sitting drinking a coffee in Phil's Restaurant
in Parrsboro Nova Scotia which isn't unusual
because as you know Parrsboro is where Dick lives.

Like many real good song writers, Dick
is a real shy person, he doesn't like people

to know he's famous. But he's a real nice guy
and he was getting a big kick out of my kids
who were eating pancakes and syrup and making a
lot of noise—

Then in came this big potbellied cigarsmoking U.S.
tourist and his nasty little wife
and they started to out-shout my kids.
They ordered breakfast and wanted to wash
their clothes in the laundromat
and they wanted to know all about Dick Elliott
not knowing he was sitting right there.

Well the proprietor, Mr. Phillips, told them
Dick writes songs under different names
and the U.S. tourist yelled out "that's for
income tax purposes." And he thought Dick
should sign up with RCA Victor. "You got
RCA Victor up here haven't you?"

And before you could say Dick Elliott, Dick Elliott
took off.

Later I asked Mr. Phillips how come Dick Elliott
is so shy. And he said Dick was brought up
in a lighthouse and married a widow.

Low Tide at Noel

Where the French drove out the Micmacs
and the British drove out the French
and even today there are mysterious fires
such as the fire that burned down the
lighthouse here—
                    and Mrs. Scott shows me
a postcard depicting high and low tide
with the gone-forever lighthouse still standing

and a farmboy drinking a can of cold blood

as he walks along the lonely road
says as he passes "Good day! Looks like rain!"

My small daughter and I hold hands
as we walk along the red sands and tidal flats
studded with boulders of unspeakable hue
such as ivory, lime, primrose and fleshy pink
and the tiny delicate shells from Cobequid Bay.

We look behind and see my large footprints
and Jenny's small footprints
that will be submerged and obliterated
in three hours but ever-fresh in my mind.

"Will you remember walking along this lonely shore
with me when you are all grown up?" I ask,
stupidly blinking away a tear

and Jenny with the innocence of a six year old
says "I think so—but when I'm all grown up
you'll be dead."

And the waters of Cobequid Bay I think
remember others now dead who left footprints
along these tidal flats, broken lovers, exiles,
although you'd never know it to look at them
being dragged in and dragged out every six hours
with stupid regularity and spewing out
life like a god.

The Invention of Gunpowder

The crazy castrated cat called Al
sat crouched in front of a brick wall
as if about to leap
              through it
while slowly a crowd of kids
gathered to watch and jeer
hoping to see him crack his skull

reminding me of that crazy Zen monk
who sat staring at a brick wall
for forty years
and when his eyelids began to droop
he cut them off
while out of the crowd of mocking monks
I stepped
picked up the eyelids
and buried them

Anyway the cat finally lay down
and fell asleep without cracking his skull
and the eyelids took root
and grew into gunpowder plants

The Canadians and the Russians 1974
Game 2, Toronto

Gordie Howe's mind is a blank but his eyes sparkle
He wishes he was fishing off his yacht in the Caribbean

Bobby Hull in his new wig looks ten years younger but he worries
that someday he will skate out on the ice and no one will cheer

Frank Mahovlich is full of hate, his stomach aches
with visions of murdered ancestors,
he wants to score ten goals for Croatia
and each time he fails he becomes more and more calm

The Russians look homesick

They are in that other huge northern country
They do not know everything
but they know they are among madmen
who do not love their land

madmen, each of whom is his own little land

Moose Jaw

Every night during the winter a wild dog
comes in off the prairie and freezes to death
in downtown Moose Jaw

Every day during the winter a Moose Jaw school kid
gets his tongue stuck to a door knob

In Moose Jaw there are scores
of tough young hockey players destined for fame

In Moose Jaw there are quite a few
unknown writers destined to remain
unknown outside of Moose Jaw

In Moose Jaw there is a chapter
of the Wilson McDonald Society
and there are still a few elderly women
who wish they'd tried harder to seduce
the grouchy young writer from Port Dover
who died saying being a poet is hell

There are several Moose Jaw novelists
who have never been as far as Saskatoon

They mail their manuscripts to publishing houses
in Toronto and never get a reply

In Moose Jaw there are dozens of poets
who sit in their warm living rooms
gazing out at the howling winters
their ordinary looking heads full of vision

and at 11 p.m. the Moose Jaw poet sets his alarm
and goes to bed and tries to ignore the strange sounds
coming from the rec room where his daughter
is entertaining the visiting poet from the east

The Angel

I

Dear friend
for several weeks
I've tried to avoid writing
but tonight I read three little poems of yours
and saw you sitting in your lonely house at 3 a.m.
in a large city 3,000 miles away
writing

words lifting out of your
unselfish heart

and my own heart melted

and I opened the dusty door of my writing room
and wrote the above
then went out and made coffee
and returned and wrote the following

for there are many reasons for writing
and only one is acceptable

for it has come to pass
that everyone can read and write
and every day we abuse
the language
that was given us
by the poets

II

I started writing the day I was born
and even now when my face has finally
begun to lose its boyishness
I find I have little to say
and little understanding of why
I continue
and I saw you sitting by your brown globe

in the twentieth century
writing

not bothering to ask why
of the gentle spirits around you

    III

I was driving along the 401
driving to the university
to give a poetry reading

but the centuries pressed in
and I was driving my old one-horse wagon
to market with a load of magic potatoes
from my magic garden

and today the old blind violinist
who stands on street corners in town
with his tin cup
died

for thought is cheap and endless
and perhaps if he had thought about it
he would have quit in disgust
and applied for a pension

forgetting the child's terror
not wanting to pass the old man by
and having no money for the cup

so he taps the bottom of the cup
hoping the blind man will think
he'd received another coin

but he taps it a little too hard
and the coins from the cup
fly up in the air
and fall to the sidewalk

and the blind man continues
playing his sad violin

IV

Stop the bus
I'm going to be sick
my brother would call out
and he would get off the bus
and he would vomit at the side of the road
then get back on proudly
age 9

I never got sick on the bus

Today a short fat woman
in a short black skirt
and a short black jacket
got sick on the bus
I felt some meanness inside me
when she pushed her way on the bus
in front of me
but my meanness went away
and I began wondering
if her ancestors and mine
had ever met
when I looked around and saw
she was about to be sick

She vomitted in the aisle
and no one said a word

I was sitting with a book in my hand
my finger marking my page
and I forgot the book
knowing only my finger was in something
important
was stopping something dreadful from
happening
was preventing further language
abuse
and she vomitted in the aisle
as if my finger had been in her throat

When I got off the bus another man
got off the bus and I walked behind him

watching his black shoes
moving along in the bright white snow
like typing on a page
knowing he too saw the woman vomit
and hoping it didn't bother him

      V

For several weeks
poems I did not like
poems that made me sick
poems I didn't want to write
passed through my mind
like annoying pop songs

I met a literary gentleman
who said
"But Irving Layton's poems are so pithy"
and I objected saying
some of them are passable
only later realizing
he wasn't lisping

I read several books by poets
striving for pithiness

I felt like a lonely ant in an anthill

Beethoven's symphonies sounded
like squadrons of trained ants

People looked like ants

They talked like ants

They moved in swarms like ants

The ants were everywhere

I watched U.S. comics on TV
mocking Russian ants
and Arab ants

and congratulating themselves
for being able to laugh
at their own antics

I saw how corrupt I was

I read three little poems by you
and an angel came out of my heart

The Wound

The beautiful young woman was severely injured
I carried her off the road and placed her
on the grassy bank of a clear deep cold stream
I put her legs in the water and lowered her jeans
She had a deep wound across her lower abdomen
I gently pushed her entrails back into the wound
Three doctors floated downstream on a raft
They smiled knowingly and complimented me on my first aid
They took the woman away with them on the raft

A Knight in Dried Plums

It could have been at the Pan-American Exposition at Buffalo in 1901. Or perhaps the Paris Exposition in 1900. Or maybe even the World's Fair at Chicago in 1893.

At any rate it was mounted proudly on a pedestal forty feet high in the centre of the main floor of the California building. A knight in dried plums.

You could get a good view of it from the balcony. There seemed to be supernatural light around it as if ghosts of knights of the past were being attracted to it like bees to the last rose of summer.

As far as is known only one writer of the time thought it worthy of mention. Here is what he wrote. "This masterpiece of ingenuity was found in the California building and reminded one of the enormous growth in the dried fruit business which is rapidly enriching the beautiful Pacific coast."

Presumably it was dismantled at the end of the fair.

It was a humble effort among the massive marble sculptures in classical form that were meant to last forever. And the mighty monuments to technology, the triumphal causeways, the stunning electric towers, the awe-inspiring cascades and the enormous engines of destruction.

The pedestal was probably to discourage people from plucking the dried plums and eating them.

from The Poet's Progress

XIII

There are colours I cannot name,
there is one now
hanging from the ceiling.

I can't describe the tie
hanging from the doorknob,

the door slightly ajar
and a red sweater
extending from the closet's darkness
like a tongue—

What is that unearthly
glorious light? Is it part
of Mecca's Sacred Shrine? No,
it is the sewing machine, my wife
silent and the woman
has failed to shut it off—

There are other things in this room.
There is me for instance.
There is Jesus, Joseph and Mary

hanging on the wall, Mary is gazing
at Jesus, and Joseph is trying to peer
down Mary's dress, and there is the sound
of the TV where a man is reciting this poem.

There is a book on Pyramids.
There is a bicycle. There is a
red hanky I could tell a funny
story about and probably will
after this poem is finished.

There is something I can't quite
put my finger on. No,
that left the room
as soon as I mentioned it
even though I didn't mention it.

Each word as I write it
comes into this room.
Perhaps somewhere in some
other room these very words
are disappearing, this poem
being unwritten, losing
a word at a time
quickly then slowly
at varying speeds
from end to beginning—

A chair is here
right where the last person
to touch it put it
unless the cat which is
not in this room but
has been
brushed against it with
enough force to move it
into its present position
from its past position
(and everything she says
has six or seven meanings,
all of them painful)
but that is not likely
since it's a heavy chair

and a light cat
too sensible to waste
energy moving this chair
that is not here
(these words are here)
and has been moved
many times
and in each place it's been
it has stayed for varying
lengths of time
perhaps as much as ten years
in one spot at one time
since it is an old chair.

It moved!
Not by itself although it
would be possible
to write that
but rather someone
came into the room
and moved it
the chair not the room
slightly then
went out too fast
for me to see but I see
the chair has moved
slightly.

What colour is the chair?
It is a sandy shade but
smoother, reflecting
the light from the sacred
sewing machine.

It is the colour of pine
smoothly sanded
once growing in a
Nova Scotia forest.

The chair
is there.
The words are
here.

I am here, there
and everywhere, a poem
that can only be defined
by other poems, a focus
of nature's benevolence,
hostility, that can only
be located by others.

There is a bottle of beer
in this room but there
is no bottle.
The beer is inside me,
the empty bottle is
outside me
and this room
but inside another
room
and inside a case
of other bottles
some capped and containing
beer and some empty
like I will be after the beer
is no longer inside me.

Please beer with me.

There is hair in this room.
It is on various parts
of my body's surface
growing out of it,
rooted into it
like tiny trees in a
Nova Scotia forest.

Prince George Express
for Gerry Gilbert and David Young

You have to be brave
to be an engineer on the British Columbia Railway
formerly known as the PGE which stood for
Pacific Great Eastern or maybe Prince George Express.
Back here in the coach our hearts beat wildly
as a wild tumultuous alpine stream plunges
down between two mountains floating on the mist
but we tend to forget the awesome responsibilities
of the man up there at the front
which is what they used to call that line of brave men
who did the actual fighting as opposed to merely killing
in the war that will never end.

So there's a frozen lake
the only flat thing in the province
(except for the skinny girl across from me who is slyly
watching me write and thinking could that be Stompin' Tom Connors?)
and there's a crazy wolf running across it
towards the train. Why is he running?
A bald eagle is chasing him. Perhaps the eagle
wants the wolf's fur to make a toupee. Anyway
the wolf is frantic, knows his only chance
is to beat the train to point X
which is the point just before the train
enters the tunnel. If he doesn't make it
he will either have to turn and run
all the way across to the far shore
or try to fight the eagle
and the eagle is big and scary
and has huge black wings like something
unspeakably unholy
                    and could probably
wrap them around that unlucky wolf
and smother him for though the wolf
is big the eagle is bigger (try putting
the CN Tower beside that mountain).

And just as sure
as the CN Tower and that mountain

will return to common clay some day
the engineer saw that old wolf
on a suicide course, better to be killed
by the Prince George Express
that have to fight that awful eagle,
and he wanted to slam on the brakes
but he knew the passengers would be
bounced around and there was a good chance
some anti-wolfite in the crowd (crowd?
there were only seven of us)
might file an official complaint
and the engineer might lose his job
as he already has several reprimands
on file (the engineer's thoughts
streaming back to me like smoke from the
stack)
   so he merely subtly slowed
down a little hoping the wolf would manage
to put on a last-minute burst of speed
and I ran over to the other side
of the coach to see if the wolf made it
and the skinny girl who hadn't noticed
the wolf thought I was about to pounce on her
and then the train entered
the tunnel and everything went dark.

I don't know to this day if the wolf made it
or if he too entered the long dark tunnel
with an instant explosion of death.

And I guess all you hunters, trappers,
woodsmen, biologists, and amateur naturalists
are laughing at this know-nothing poet
and yes I must admit the engineer later laughed
and told me that was no wolf
that was a coyote
     and the bald eagle
wasn't chasing him, they were merely
fighting over a hunk of rotting meat
somewhere out on the frozen lake
and he also said the coyote
made it with *lots* of room to spare

and he denied slowing down to avoid
hitting him

and as they say in confessional novels
something beautiful went out of my life
and though I hate him for spoiling
the magic of this tale I'll still tell it
to my kids when and if I get home

and I still say you have to be brave
to be an engineer on the BC Railway,
you never know when you're going to
come around a bend at forty and find
a rock lying on the track—

In fact round about 100 Mile House
lying on a small plain
is a rock as big as a *house*
that fell off a mountain 100 miles away
and just kept rolling till it stopped
next to the railroad and though it probably
happened several thousand years
before the railroad was built
it could probably happen again
(by the way, in case you didn't get it
that's why they call it *100 Mile House*).

Mock on Voltaire, Rousseau
I still say you have to be brave
to be a poet.

        And so
a little while later up around
the little town of Williams Lake
I got thinking about how brave
a poet has to be, forever searching
for original ideas and weird experiences
(without making it obvious of course)
and I got feeling kind of brave myself
so when the girl handing out sandwiches and tea
lost her balance and fell on me
and I caught her and she looked up

into my one good eye and said thanks
that would have been a nasty fall
how can I ever thank you, I looked back
into her one good eye and said
there is a way you can thank me you know
and she looked pleased and said how?
I paused then hissed out this cold-blooded refrain:
Ask the engineer to let me drive the train.

Regulations prohibit passengers she said
after standing up and regaining her composure
from entering the front compartment
never mind driving the train.

Ah come on just for a few crummy miles I said,
getting braver, just for the experience I said,
the other passengers remaining strangely silent.

So she looked a little perplexed and said
oh all right I'll ask the engineer
then came back a little while later
saying the engineer says it's okay by him—
as long as you get the unanimous
consent of all the passengers

so I got up in the aisle and made an
eloquent plea for unanimity—

Can you wait until Quesnel?
yelled out one guy—

Can you wait until Woodpecker?
yelled out another—

Can you wait until Cinema?
said a little voice—

Oh are you from Cinema? said I.
Is there a movie theatre there?

The guy thought hard for a minute
then said no I'm pretty sure there isn't.

Then I got talking to young Bob Thompson
who had just lost his job as an oiler
on the railroad at his home in Shalaith
where he owns two horses, one quarterhorse
and a fourteen-year-old named Candy
with real short legs who nabbed fourth place
out of a field of two hundred and fifty
in a mountain race with Bob in the saddle
and Bob said he often entered amateur rodeos
as a bareback rider but he wasn't very good
and he was always being thrown
and almost always landed on his head
and he said his Uncle Walter in Lillooet
had just bought a $2,500
snowmobile which could go eighty miles an hour
uphill
        and Bob was going to Prince George
to try to get a job as an oiler on the railroad
the same railroad he'd just been fired from
and I guess that made sense
and I asked why he didn't apply
to be an engineer on the railroad
and Bob looked a little sick and said
you have to be really brave
to be an engineer on the PGE
even braver than you have to be
to join the rodeo
        because in a rodeo
all you're killing is yourself
but if you do something wrong on the PGE—
get drunk, misread a signal, fall asleep—
you could kill six or seven people
and then again they have to take too much
guff to suit me said Bob, his sleepy eyes
and shy smile set off by a range
of volcanic pimples.

And as the Prince George Express picked up speed
past Soda Creek heading north into the night
I asked Bob if there were many accidents
on the railroad.
        Oh yeah
lots of them he said. A lot of times

a logging truck will lose its brakes
flying down a mountain road and hit the train
broadside
        and it almost always
happens along this stretch right here.

And I slumped down in my seat
and closed my eyes to prepare for possible death
and I could hear Bob going on
as if I were still listening, going on
about Rene Levesque, a submicroscopic dot
hidden behind a thousand eastern horizons.
All those people in Quebec who don't like
Canada should go back to Paris or France
or one of those places he said.
I've only been as far as Saskatoon Saskatchewan
he said but I want to go down and have a look
at Ontario some day. I love this country.
If Quebec wants to split up I'd go to war
to stop them. In fact if British Columbia
wanted to leave Canada I'd go to Alberta
and join the army and I'd even shoot my own
neighbours to keep this country together—
and I opened my eyes and looked into his
and he looked back and smiled softly
and he asked me if I knew where Oklahoma was
and I said yes, it's in the central part
of the United States of America. Why?
We were talking to someone from Oklahoma
the other day on our little CB radio he said.
Usually we can only talk to people
no more than twenty miles away—
and he wanted me to explain why all of a sudden
they could make contact with Oklahoma—

And even though I had to disappoint him
by admitting I didn't have a clue why they suddenly
could get Oklahoma he still said he was going to come
to Hamilton Ontario some day and look me up

and the skinny girl across the aisle said
Hamilton Ontario? Did somebody say Hamilton Ontario?
That's where I'm from.

And I thought (to myself)
you have to be brave
to be a passenger on the British Columbia Railway.

How I Came to Understand Irving Layton

On a plane flying into Calgary
I found myself sitting next to a
blonde, blue-eyed, six-foot-tall
seventy-year-old Mennonite lady
    of stern visage
who tried to bring her simplistic
fanatic notions about Christianity
into every attempt
at ordinary conversation.
I'm going to have to start sitting
in the smoking section I thought.

She'd spent all her life caring
for her infirm mother, now ninety,
and was returning from the funeral
in Owen Sound of her uncle
who was struck down in action,
died while broadcasting a hellfire
sermon all over the Bruce Peninsula
and now presumably was hectoring
all the angels in heaven.

She wanted to know what I did for a living
and when I said I was a writer
she wanted to know what I wrote about
and she got a little flustered
when I told her I like to write
about ordinary everyday things
like descriptions of the people
I meet on planes

and she wanted to know if I believed
in the Life Hereafter and I said you bet
and she said that's what makes

life worthwhile, isn't it?
and I said oh I can think of other things
that make life worthwhile
and she looked at me as if she wasn't
quite sure what I meant but wanted me to know
if I meant what she thought I meant
she never did those things

so I figured I ought to turn the occasion
into a self-educational opportunity
and I asked her to fill me in
on the history of the Mennonites

and she got embarrassed
and said she didn't know much about history
being more interested
in praying and serving Jesus Christ
in her daily life
or something

but she did say they were from Germany
and she did say there were still quite
a few Mennonites living in Germany

and so I asked her if the Mennonites
were persecuted in the war,
if the ones who were in Germany
when Hitler came to power
tried to stop him, were sent
to the ovens and all that
or did they just stay silent
like Richard Strauss

and she said she didn't know,
no one had ever given her any data
on that
      although I later found out
thousands were martyred in Europe
in the sixteenth century and 80
per cent of all the conscientious objectors
in Canada in World War II
were Mennonites

but she said she'd rather
just talk about Jesus Christ,
all this talk about different
religious denominations
was a bit overdone, didn't I think?
Who cares? she said as a dark cloud
passed over her face. Who cares . . .
as long as you're Christian?

Although I almost always abstain
from meddling in the beliefs of others
something in her voice just hit me
and I began yelling so loud
I almost woke the pilot.
What? I cried. I couldn't stop myself.
What about Jews? What about Arabs?
What about Buddhists, Hindus, Sikhs
and Rastafarians?

I looked at her. She looked a little
uncomfortable. Her eyes looked
frightened, as if the ship she'd
been sailing on all her life
had suddenly been torpedoed
and was sinking fast.

And abruptly a look of relief, of pleasure,
came into her softening blue eyes as if for the
first time in her life she realized
that all that crap she'd been taught
about non-Christians being heathens,
less than human, doomed to eternal damnation,
was wrong
and all the tiny muscles in her face
began to relax

and I looked into her eyes again
and I could see them sliding into
a third phase, the phase in which
she suddenly realized not only Christ
was God, but all of us are God, even Jews,
and I thought I detected a halo-like glow
forming around her head

and she loosened up and began
enjoying the beautiful moment all around her
for the first time in years

and the heavens parted and a beautiful
dove flew down and landed on her head

and she moved over closer to me
and I could feel the long-neglected
warmth of love radiating from her breast

and even I felt great all over
and I began thinking about Irving Layton
devoting his poetic life to destroying
all this puerile Sunday School
steeltrap Christianity

and suddenly for the first time
I understood my brother Irving

and suddenly I saw how enjoyable
it must be for the old guy

and how easy it would be
to get hooked on it

and hooked bad.

For Barbara

Barbara, put down your flute
and pay attention.

A motorcyclist in the high Andes
has been forced off the road
and is falling...

Quick!
Do something!

The Rockies

When we walk to the horizon
we are amazed to find things
as small as they seemed
    —Robert Fones

No wonder the gods are so aloof
and also politicians who fly a lot
said I with sorrow
as I sat sipping Air Canada reserve
German wine
and listening to the mighty Ninth Symphony
30,000 feet above the Rockies.

Perhaps a party of ant-like climbers
is stranded on one of those puny
ice-capped peaks far below,
the wind howling, food gone, no hope
but to sink into eternal sleep.

I'm going to stop looking out the window
this gives the wrong perspective on things
I thought then started looking down again—
God, if Hitler could have seen these views
he probably would have killed more Jews.

The stewardess stops and I ask her
for help with the crossword puzzle
and compliment her on the wonderful
stereo selections, and I suggest
Air Canada black out the windows
for this kind of looking down on the world
is okay for great novelists like Tolstoy or Hardy
but what can it do for ordinary folk like me
but bring out our latent cruelty
and she laughs and walks away

and what if that flimsy wing suddenly
snapped under the awful pressure I presume
is out there?
             Would I remain calm
as the plane plummeted down?

Of course you would, immortal bard,
murmurs my agreeable frontal lobe
while somewhere at the back of my brain
a woman's voice, the voice of the future, whispers
You'd fall to pieces long before you hit the ground
and I for one would be glad to see that happen.

My Body Was Eaten by Dogs

I met her while walking in Egypt
on the road to Oxyrhynchus
where the Ibycus papyrus was found.
Her body had been eaten by dogs,
torn into little pieces,
each piece
        still glowing with life.

How I met her, I tripped on the road
then noticed the rock that caught my toe
was a face,
        a large broken nose and a
once-smooth chin cracked and chipped.

She looked up at me with hardened eyes
silently pleading to be picked up

and I wondered what it would be like
to spend centuries without a workable body,
life clinging to small fragments of petrified flesh
like reflections to pieces of shattered glass.

And there she was lying like a rock
in the road, helpless, a living
rock among all the other rocks,
a living planet searching the heavens
for signs of life.

And finally as I hesitated wondering
if I had time to waste on this, this . . .
I mean it was a curious situation all right

but the landscape was loaded, overloaded
with equally curious situations
and I was in a hurry to reach the sea

and the strange black mouth opened
and I had a glimpse of the awful warmth
of a life that has nothing else
but warmth.

My body, she said,
was eaten by dogs.

And her mouth slowly closed again
like a clam with a morsel to digest
and she continued staring up at me
as if I were the first person
in five thousand years
to have noticed her lying on the road

and I picked her up
and put her in my bag
and eventually brought her back to Canada

and now she is sitting on my bookshelf
in my log cabin in Tuktoyaktuk
and every nine minutes or so
she opens her mouth to say
My body was eaten by dogs

and her shrunken, blue-grey eyes
never close.

Hsu Fu's Speech to the Five Hundred Youths of Both Sexes*

The emperor's mind is plagued by thoughts
of sickness and accident befalling his children
as the mind of the lover is entered
when least expected by thoughts
of the loss of the beloved
and the thoughts are so painful
they make the lover wish he'd never loved.

The Emperor Shih-huang
has unified all of China
and has constructed the Great Wall
to keep out the barbarians
but he can build nothing to keep
thoughts of the deaths of his loved ones
from stealing into his mind.

I did not invent these stories
of the miraculous *ling chih*.
I had it on good account
that it grew on the Isle of Tsu
in the Eastern Sea,
a plant that lives forever and in turn
confers eternal life on those who eat it,
a plant shaped like water-grass
with blades four feet long,
food for the hungry mind,
rest for the restless spirit,
peace for the tortured king.

And because of my regard for the emperor
I told him I had heard
that a man three days dead
revives immediately
when the plant is merely placed upon him

---

*Under the reign of Shih-huang, founder of the Ch'in Dynasty (221-206 B.C.), the shaman Hsu Fu rallied five hundred youths of both sexes to sail to the southeast looking for the fabled *ling chih*. According to one account they never returned. It's been suggested they landed on the west coast of Vancouver Island.

and he asked me if I thought it would work
on a prince fallen from a horse
or a princess felled by sudden illness.

All I could tell him was what I had heard:
that the plant works with murdered people
for when murder victims lay in the Great Preserve
huge black birds with these leaves in their bills
flew down and placed them on the corpses' faces
and the murdered people sat up and smiled.

And I told him the Doctor of the Spectre Valley
called it the herb of immortality
that grows on the Isle of Tsu
in the Eastern Sea
in red marble fields
one stalk sufficing to save a man's life
and the look that came over Shih-huang-ti's face
was one of sudden delight.
"Can we get to it from here?" he said.

And the sage Lu-Sheng told the king
the plant was a supernatural mushroom
that grows on mountaintops
a fungus with miraculous properties
and advised the king he should travel alone
into the mountains, quietly, under disguise
and the fungus might be surprised
into yielding its immortality.

And someone, it might have been me,
spoke of the islands of the Eastern Sea
where bright palaces made from *ling chih*
illuminated all the heavens
and the servants were copper in colour
and dragon-like in appearance.

And the king called me privately
and told me to build a ship with wooden decks
and choose five hundred youths of either sex
to sail away to the Isle of Tsu
and bring back a goodly harvest of the plant.

And so my young friends we've explored
the Isle of Tsu and the other two
godly islands in the Eastern Sea
and have found nothing that would resemble
in any form the miraculous *ling chih*,
no water grass with stalks four feet long,
no fungus with supernatural properties,
no nine-stemmed mushrooms with twin caps,
and in the clouds in the western skies
I see the emperor's tearful eyes
searching for us in his mind.

I know you want to return to your homeland
but I'm sure you'll understand if I'm reluctant
to come before the good emperor once again
and tell him I have found no trace
of the divine plant of endless grace.

So I have a proposal to make.
Let us sail further into the rising sun
into seas uncharted and unexplored,
let us keep sailing forever and a day
visiting all the lands we meet in the east
until we find what we are looking for
until we find what will please the emperor
and let us pledge never to return
let us pledge to sail and sail eternally
until we find the plant of immortality.

Fingers

She holds up three fingers
and says *That really does
look like a W doesn't it Daddy?*

She tells me she's writing
a story about India
which has the largest
continuous farmland

and the highest mountains
which are called *The Land of the Snow.*

I look into her eyes
and for a moment
I know her future agony
as if looking in a mirror.

Later alone in my room
thinking of my present agony
I hold up one finger like a gun
point it at my head
and say *Bang!*

And somewhere out in the kitchen
one daughter says to the other
Did you hear a bang?

Border Skirmish

In a laundromat
in the east end
of Hamilton
Ontario
at 7:30
on a Sunday morning
a lovely lady named Joan
runs out of change and so
runs across the street
to the McDonald Hamburgatorium
standing now where once stood
the house where she was born.

She hands the woman a five
and asks for change for the laundry machines
and the woman is kind of bitchy
and says I can't give you no change
I need all I got
as if anyone who would be out of change
on a Sunday morning

in the east end
of Hamilton
Ontario
is some kind of degenerate

Shee-it (says Joan) a billion burgers
you've sold in this once-proud land
and you can't even change a five
to help a native in a Sunday morning jam
—Okay then give me a cup of tea

We don't have tea
says the woman
superiorly
(tea being basically
an unamerican drink)
then give me a cup of coffee says Joan
who never drinks coffee
and she hands the woman the five
and the woman looks a little sick
as if the founder of the firm
is looking over her shoulder
and has caught her with her finger
up her bum
or up somebody else's bum
but what can she do
nothing
so she hands over a coffee
and two twos
and three quarters in change

So Joan with a funny little smile
hands the woman back one of the twos
and says now I'd like an orange juice
and the woman thinks to herself
oh shit
but what can she do
nothing
so she hands over the orange juice
and a one
and three quarters in change

So Joan with the same little smile
gives the woman the other two
and says now I'd like a Danish
and the woman's eyes roll up to heaven
or what passes for heaven in McDonaldland
and her face turns bright red
and her wig starts bouncing up and down
but what could she do
nothing
so she hands over the Danish
and another one
and three quarters

So now in case you haven't been counting
Joan has managed to get nine quarters
in change out of McDonald's
enough to do all her laundry
in the east end
of Hamilton
Ontario
at 7:30
on a Sunday morning

a small victory really
just barely worth recording in verse
because she's paid for every one
of those nine quarters

oh how she's paid

1977

In Calgary under a train bridge
in 1962 a chocolate bar wrapper
came to rest in the mud

I said I'm going to remember this
fifteen years from now

and I did

The Opening of the West

Two crows and a hawk are fighting fifty feet
above the Ontario-Manitoba border
above the line where the great shield
breaks and the trees disappear.
The hills crumble into rocks
and the rocks stop and start again
and isolated stands of poplar
become fewer and smaller and shorter
like the last little islands at the
end of the earth
                  and the low winter sun
radiates everything with prairie fluorescence.

I thumbed a ride into Sioux Lookout
in a tractor trailer on a rainy midnight.
I had to help the guy deliver lumber
at various camps around the Lake of the Woods
then fell asleep in the cab
and when I awoke I looked at the driver
and he was asleep slumped over the wheel
at 60 mph. "Hey wake up!" I yelled and he jumped
then said "Just resting my eyes."

Then another rig pulled up alongside
on the two-lane Trans-Canada
and they began racing, the only
things on the road at dawn, this
flat geometric heaven
or some other supernatural zone
treeless, where you can see forever
and then when you get there
you can still see forever
or as Al Purdy says you can look
forever in any direction except down
and for amusement the angels
pick up hitchikers and race each other
across the bottom of the sky
and I got a little lonely and scared
and wondered what they were doing
back in Ontario

and I thought if I had to live here long
I'd become a mirror image of myself
and slip through a crack and vanish
which seemed a scary proposition at the time
being a rather unmetaphysical kid

and in recent years I've flown across this line
many times, noting it's not marked
on the world's largest map, that map
they unroll beneath you as you fly
and the prairies look no flatter
than the 3,650 mountains
of British Columbia

and I heard an old Inuit in Tuktoyaktuk
say he'd visited Ottawa once long ago
and it was just like a dream he sighed
a heavenly mist in his one good eye

and now yes it's just like a dream
everything that is even meeting by chance
that well-known saviour and holy man
Jesus Christ during a train stop
in Capreol which is 572 miles north
of Toronto and 635 east of Winnipeg
Winnipeg where a mysterious old African
is spending a long afternoon sipping
slow beers in a downtown pub
the same African who forty years ago
shot down Capreol Red, the most bastardly
CNR bull of the Depression,
Capreol a tiny decimal point
on which so much depends.

And now with Jesus disembarked
in Winnipeg, I promised to write
and wondered where we'd meet next time,
the sun is setting west of Brandon
setting right in my face
and my upper torso is all aglow
not to mention my lower,
I wished I'd taken notes on the
endless stream of stories Christ told

protesting he's not a teetotaller
I mean a good storyteller
we all know he's not a teetotaller
although he tries to go easy these days
because of an ulcer condition, and nights,
and he's not supposed to eat
anything with seeds—
God, Christ told some great stories
and great imitations of Pierre Trudeau
and of an Indian woman
who sounded just like Victoria Reindeer
of Fort Smith
                Jesus became
the spirit of the prairies to me
and I told him about meeting a guy
who said he liked to take his horse
and spend weeks loping around the
      Cypress Hills
shooting rattlesnakes and eating them
after roasting them over hot prairie coals
in the evening with the western sky
changing colours

and Jesus said rattlesnake? Why rattlesnake?
There's a lot of prairie chicken in them
     Cypress Hills

and he said how in Sioux the word *manitou*
means both God and Prairie
and how even the Indians were somewhat
alienated from the land
and had to use animals as intercessors
much as Christians use himself.

And I saw young Jesus growing into
some kind of narrative sage (if he lived)
long done with the foolishness
     of holiness
and we looked similar, talked
almost the same although born
almost a world apart
and each of us in his way

tampers with the boundaries
between history and life

yet the epic wanderings of Paul Kane
and the everrotting corpse of Louis Riel
lie in him, not me,
and the great buffalo herds spring
back to life in him, not me

and he kept talking about how he
almost didn't take this train from Ottawa
where he was guest speaker at a convention
of descendants of the Chinese coolies
who built the great Canadian railroad
and how various coincidences developed
that made it impossible to take the one
he wanted, his grey eyes holding mine

and we embraced and I confessed
that at the funeral of a dear friend
a few days before, a death
that for two nights had kept me awake
more than the train's rocking and whistling
I had regretted never having embraced him
and never having told him
how much I loved him
in a completely asexual way of course
because I was afraid he'd think it
queer
    and Jesus, though slightly
embarrassed, returned the embrace
and talked of how he embraced his father
after a long absence

and he spoke of how all this public speaking
was developing into a chore

and how he's getting sick of catching
small fish in the Rockies around Banff
and how he wanted to come to Northern Ontario
specifically the million lakes north of Sioux Lookout
and try to catch a twenty-pound rainbow trout

and just then the West opened up

and a tight flock of birds so high
they looked like a cluster of decimal points
suddenly scattered.

Lennox Island

They're more beautiful than the angels of heaven
the beautiful Micmac children of Lennox Island
as all through the long summer they dive dive dive
off the dock into the warm waters of Malpeque Bay.
Sometimes they join hands and leap in en masse
then resurface with a gasp, dark hair streaming
and dark eyes flashing in the sun.
From early morning to early evening they dive,
careful to avoid the poisonous jellyfish
which they sometimes call bloodsuckers
and pick like giant mushrooms and flip onto the dock
to die, to fry in the hot sun like eggs,
the dock coated with fading remains
of the summer's harvest and stains
of previous summers.   It's hard to believe
there are children on earth more beautiful
than the beautiful Micmac children of Lennox Island,
aristocratic, oriental, magical and shining with joy.
As for me the water is too full of bloodsuckers
and the current too strong for me to swim
and I remain silent, strained, and wish I could vanish
for fear they'll flee or become somehow tainted
by my clumsy, poisonous presence
and so I strive to become relatively pure
and I invite life to flow through my body
as it flows through the bodies of these children
but I simply become more and more aware
of my powers of destruction and I quietly leave.

And I believe these children are my ancestors
and I believe these children populated the once-sacred earth

and I believe Lennox Island and across the bay
Bird Island, Hog Island, and maybe even part of the
Prince Edward Island mainland
is the birthplace of the human race
and I believe that since that glorious day
we've become more and more stupid in every way.

But I'm not about to immolate myself
because of the imminent death of an ancient race
and I'm thankful fate has given me a glimpse
of all this beauty before it's gone forever.
And on a hill overlooking the dock where the children play
is a curiously twisted hunk of metal.
It is a World War I cannon
that appears to have suffered a direct hit
and there is a plaque to the memory
of the nine Lennox Island men
who were killed in that horrible white man's war
that war that failed to destroy
that widely held belief in Caucasian superiority
except in the minds of non-Caucasians.

And standing quietly watching me
as I try to swallow my foolish tears
is a tall young man of pure African descent
who tells me he's a student from Calgary
who volunteered to spend the summer working
with the 200 Micmac residents of Lennox Island
and he tells me the Micmacs of Lennox Island
are a shy people who desire as little contact as possible
with white occupants of Prince Edward Island
but they're an industrious group of people
who are perhaps the world's best oyster farmers
and he predicted the beautiful children on the dock
would eventually leave Lennox Island
for Summerside, Charlottetown,
or maybe even Halifax or Moncton,
but they would return after a short time
disillusioned, sick in spirit
and spend the rest of their lives on Lennox Island.

On the Road Again

It's all part of growing up.
I know Canada is the only country in the world
    more American than the U.S.A.
We're so stupid we accept Colonel Sanders and reject
    Frank O'Hara.
But I was sitting at the bar in a pub in Carleton Place
    at 6 p.m. on Tuesday, April 6 1976, just before the
    Stompin' Tom Connors concert in Smiths Falls.
The guys were talking about their snowmobiles.
Suddenly it happened.
In spite of the ugliness of so much of our history, our
    culture and our lives, ugliness that will probably
    never end, I felt at home.
My heart, normally the size of a dried plum, grew to fill
    the room, the town, the province, the whole damned
    country.
And these lines came bubbling up.
If I'm ever remembered, this is what I'd like to be remembered
    by:

> *Toss*
> *a dart at the map of Canada,*
> *where it lands is*
> *where you'll find me.*

Intense Pleasure

These are the days I'll remember
when we are dead.